VACATION HOMES

-Frames • Chalets • Designs 480 to 3,238 Sq. Ft.

HOME PLANNERS, INC.

Contents

Published by Home Planners, Inc., 23761 Research Drive, Farmington Hills, Michigan 48024. All designs and illustrative material Copyright ᶜ MCMLXXXVII by Home Planners, Inc. All rights reserved. Reproduction in any manner or form not permitted. Printed in the United States of America. International Standard Book Number (ISBN): 0-918894-54-9.

Index to Designs

On the Cover: Cover design can be found on page 17.

How To Read Floor Plans and Blueprints

Selecting the most suitable house plan for your family is a matter of matching your needs, tastes, and life-style against the many designs we offer. When you study the floor plans in this issue, and the blueprints that you may subsequently order, remember that they are simply a two-dimensional representation of what will eventually be a three-dimensional reality.

Floor plans are easy to read. Rooms are clearly labeled, with dimensions given in feet and inches. Most symbols are logical and self-explanatory: The location of bathroom fixtures, planters, fireplaces, tile floors, cabinets and counters, sinks, appliances, closets, sloped or beamed ceilings will be obvious.

A blueprint, although much more detailed, is also easy to read; all it demands is concentration. The blueprints that we offer come in many large sheets, each one of which contains a different kind of information. One sheet contains foundation and excavation drawings, another has a precise plot plan. An elevations sheet deals with the exterior walls of the house; section drawings show precise dimensions, fittings, doors, windows, and roof structures. Our detailed floor plans give the construction information needed by your contractor. And each set of blueprints contains a lengthy materials list with size and quantities of all necessary components. Using this list, a contractor and suppliers can make a start at calculating costs for you.

When you first study a floor plan or blueprint, imagine that you are walking through the house. By mentally visualizing each room in three dimensions, you can transform the technical data and symbols into something more real.

Start at the front door. It's preferable to have a foyer or entrance hall in which to receive guests. A closet here is desirable; a powder room is a plus.

Look for good traffic circulation as you study the floor plan. You should not have to pass all the way through one main room to reach another. From the entrance area you should have direct access to the three principal areas of a house—the living, work, and sleeping zones. For example, a foyer might provide separate entrances to the living room, kitchen, patio, and a hallway or staircase leading to the bedrooms.

Study the layout of each zone. Most people expect the living room to be protected from cross traffic. The kitchen, on the other hand, should connect with the dining room—and perhaps also the utility room, basement, garage, patio or deck, or a secondary entrance. A homemaker whose workday centers in the kitchen may have special requirements: a window that faces the backyard; a clear view of the family room where children play; a garage or driveway entrance that

allows for a short trip with groceries; laundry facilities close hand. Check for efficient placement of kitchen cabine counters, and appliances. Is there enough room in the kitche for additional appliances, for eating in? Is there a dining nook

Perhaps this part of the house contains a family room or den/bedroom/office. It's advantageous to have a bathroom powder room in this section.

As you study the plan, you may encounter a staircas indicated by a group of parallel lines, the number of lin equaling the number of steps. Arrows labeled "up" mean th the staircase leads to a higher level, and those pointing dow mean it leads to a lower one. Staircases in a split-level w have both up and down arrows on one staircase because tw levels are depicted in one drawing and an extra level another.

Notice the location of the stairways. Is too much floor spa lost to them? Will you find yourself making too many trips?

Study the sleeping quarters. Are the bedrooms situated you like? You may want the master bedroom near the kids, you may want it as far away as possible. Is there at least o closet per person in each bedroom or a double one for couple? Bathrooms should be convenient to each bedroom— not adjoining, then with hallway access and on the same flo

Once you are familiar with the relative positions of t rooms, look for such structural details as:

• Sufficient uninterrupted wall space for furniture arrang ment.

• Adequate room dimensions.

• Potential heating or cooling problems—i.e., a room over garage or next to the laundry.

• Window and door placement for good ventilation a natural light.

• Location of doorways—avoid having a basement staircase a bathroom in view of the dining room.

• Adequate auxiliary space—closets, storage, bathroom countertops.

• Separation of activity areas. (Will noise from the recreati room disturb sleeping children or a parent at work?)

As you complete your mental walk through the house, be in mind your family's long-range needs. A good house pla will allow for some adjustments now and additions in t future.

Each member of your family may find the listing of his, her, favorite features a most helpful exercise. Why not try i

How To Choose a Contractor

A contractor is part craftsman, part businessman, and part magician. As the person who will transform your dreams and drawings into a finished house, he will be responsible for the total cost of the structure, for the quality of the workmanship, and for the solving of all problems that occur quite naturally in the course of construction. Choose him as carefully as you would a business partner, because for the next several months that will be his role in your life.

As soon as you have a building site and house plans, start looking for a contractor, even if you do not plan to break ground for several months. Finding one suitable to build your house can take time, and once you have found him, you will have to be worked into his schedule. Those who are good are in demand and, where the season is short, they are often scheduling work up to a year in advance.

There are two types of residential contractors: the construction company and the carpenter-builder, often called a general contractor. Each of these has its advantages and disadvantages.

The carpenter-builder works directly on the job as the field foreman. Because his background is that of a craftsman, his workmanship is probably good—but his paperwork may be slow or sloppy. His overhead—which you pay for—is less than that of a large construction company. However, if the job drags on for any reason, his interest may flag because your project is overlapping his next job and eroding his profits.

Construction companies handle several projects concurrently. They have an office staff to keep the paperwork moving and an army of subcontractors they know they can count on. Though you can be confident that they will meet deadlines, they may sacrifice workmanship in order to do so. Because they emphasize efficiency, they are less personal to work with than a general contractor. Many will not work with an individual unless he is represented by an architect. The company and the architect speak the same language; it requires far more time to deal directly with a homeowner.

To find a reliable contractor, start by asking friends who have built homes for recommendations. Check with local lumber yards and building supply outlets for names of possible candidates.

Once you have several names in hand, ask the Chamber of Commerce, Better Business Bureau, or local department of consumer affairs for any information they might have on each of them. Keep in mind that these watchdog organizations can give only the number of complaints filed; they cannot tell you what percent of those claims were valid. Remember, too, that a large-volume operation is logically going to have more complaints against it than will an independent contractor.

Set up an interview with each of the potential candidates. Find out what his specialty is—custom houses, development houses, remodeling, or office buildings. Ask each to take you to—not just to the site of—houses he has built. Ask to see projects that are complete as well as work in progress, emphasizing that you are interested in projects comparable to yours. A $300,000 dentist's office will give you little insight into a contractor's craftsmanship.

Ask each contractor for bank references from both his commercial bank and any other lender he has worked with. If he is in good financial standing, he should have no qualms about giving you this information. Also ask if he offers a warranty on his work. Most will give you a one-year warranty on the structure; some offer as much as a ten-year warranty.

Ask for references, even though no contractor will give you the name of a dissatisfied customer. While previous clients may be pleased with a contractor's work overall, they may, for example, have had to wait three months after they moved in before they had any closet doors. Ask about his follow-through. Did he clean up the building site, or did the owner have to dispose of the refuse? Ask about his business organization. Did the paperwork go smoothly, or was there a delay in hooking up the sewer because he forgot to apply for a permit?

Talk to each of the candidates about fees. Most work on a "cost plus" basis; that is, the basic cost of the project—materials, subcontractors' services, wages of those working directly on the project, but not office help—plus his fee. Some have a fixed fee; others work on a percentage of the basic cost. A fixed fee is usually better for you if you can get one. If a contractor works on a percentage, ask for a cost breakdown of his best estimate and keep very careful track as the work progresses. A crafty contractor can always use a cost overrun to his advantage when working on a percentage.

Do not be overly suspicious of a contractor who won't work on a fixed fee. One who is very good and in great demand may not be willing to do so. He may also refuse to submit a competitive bid.

If the top two or three candidates are willing to submit competitive bids, give each a copy of the plans and your specifications for materials. If they are not each working from the same guidelines, the competitive bids will be of little value. Give each the same deadline for turning in a bid; two or three weeks is a reasonable period of time. If you are willing to go with the lowest bid, make an appointment with all of them and open the envelopes in front of them.

If one bid is remarkably low, the contractor may have made an honest error in his estimate. Do not try to hold him to it if he wants to withdraw his bid. Forcing him to build at too low a price could be disastrous for both you and him.

Though the above method sounds very fair and orderly, it is not always the best approach, especially if you are inexperienced. You may want to review the bids with your architect, if you have one, or with your lender to discuss which to accept. They may not recommend the lowest. A low bid does not necessarily mean that you will get quality with economy.

If the bids are relatively close, the most important consideration may not be money at all. How easily you can talk with a contractor and whether or not he inspires confidence are very important considerations. Any sign of a personality conflict between you and a contractor should be weighed when making a decision.

Once you have financing, you can sign a contract with the builder. Most have their own contract forms, but it is advisable to have a lawyer draw one up or, at the very least, review the standard contract. This usually costs a small flat fee.

A good contract should include the following:
• Plans and sketches of the work to be done, subject to your approval.
• A list of materials, including quantity, brand names, style or serial numbers. (Do not permit any "or equal" clause that will allow the contractor to make substitutions.)
• The terms—who (you or the lender) pays whom and when.
• A production schedule.
• The contractor's certification of insurance for workmen's compensation, damage, and liability.
• A rider stating that all changes, whether or not they increase the cost, must be submitted and approved in writing.

Of course, this list represents the least a contract should include. Once you have signed it, your plans are on the way to becoming a home.

A frequently asked question is: "Should I become my own general contractor?" Unless you have knowledge of construction, material purchasing, and experience supervising subcontractors, we do not recommend this route.

How To Shop For Mortgage Money

Most people who are in the market for a new home spend months searching for the right house plan and building site. Ironically, these same people often invest very little time shopping for the money to finance their new home, though the majority will have to live with the terms of their mortgage for as long as they live in the house.

The fact is that all banks are not alike, nor are the loans that they offer—and banks are not the only financial institutions that lend money for housing. The amount of down payment, interest rate, and period of the mortgage are all, to some extent, negotiable.

• Lending practices vary from one city and state to another. If you are a first-time builder or are new to an area, it is wise to hire a real estate (not divorce or general practice) attorney to help you unravel the maze of your specific area's laws, ordinances, and customs.

• Before talking with lenders, write down all your questions. Take notes during the conversation so you can make accurate comparisons.

• Do not be intimidated by financial officers. Keep in mind that *you are not begging for money,* you are buying it. Do not hesitate to reveal what other institutions are offering; they may be challenged to meet or better the terms.

• Use whatever clout you have. If you or your family have been banking with the same firm for years, let them know that they could lose your business if you can get a better deal elsewhere.

• Know your credit rights. The law prohibits lenders from considering only the husband's income when determining eligibility, a practice that previously kept many people out of the housing market. If you are turned down for a loan, you have a right to see a summary of the credit report and change any errors in it.

A GUIDE TO LENDERS

Where can you turn for home financing? Here is a list of sources for you to approach:

Savings and loan associations are the best place to start because they write well over half the mortgages in the United States on dwellings that house from one to four families. They generally offer favorable interest rates, require lower down payments, and allow more time to pay off loans than do other banks.

Savings banks, sometimes called mutual savings banks, are your next best bet. Like savings and loan associations, much of their business is concentrated in home mortgages.

Commercial banks write mortgages as a sideline, and when money is tight many will not write mortgages at all. They do hold about 15 percent of the mortgages in the country, however, and when the market is right, they can be very competitive.

Mortgage banking companies use the money of private investors to write home loans. They do a brisk business in government-backed loans, which other banks are reluctant to handle because of the time and paperwork required.

Some credit unions are now allowed to grant mortgages. A few insurance companies, pension funds, unions, and fraternal organizations also offer mortgage money to their membership, often at terms more favorable than those available in the commercial marketplace.

A GUIDE TO MORTGAGES

The types of mortgages available are far more various than most potential home buyers realize.

Traditional Loans

Conventional home loans have a fixed interest rate and fixed monthly payments. About 80 percent of the mortgage money in the United States is lent in this manner. Made by private lending institutions, these fixed rate loans are available to anyone whom the bank officials consider a good credit risk. The interest rate depends on the prevailing market for money and is slightly negotiable if you are willing to put down a large down payment. Most down payments range from 15 to 33 percent.

You can borrow as much money as the lender believes you can afford to pay off over the negotiated period of time—usually 20 to 30 years. However, a 15 year mortgage can save you considerably and enable you to own your home in half the time. For example, a 30 year, $60,800 mortgage at 12% interest will have a monthly payment of $625.40 per month vs $729.72 per month for a 15 year loan at the same interest rate. At the end of 30 years you have paid $164,344 in interest vs $70,550 for the 15 year. Remember - this is only $104.32 more per month. Along with saving with a 15 year mortgage, additional savings

can be realized with a biweekly payment plan. So be sure to consu your borrowing institution for all of your options.

The FHA does not write loans; it insures them against default i order to encourage lenders to write loans for first-time buyers an people with limited incomes. The terms of these loans make them ver attractive, and you may be allowed to take as long as 25 to 30 years pay it off.

The down payment also is substantially lower with an FHA-backe loan. At present it is set at 3 percent of the first $25,000 and 5 percen of the remainder, up to the $75,300 limit. This means that a loan on $75,300 house would require a $750 down payment on the first $25,00 plus $2,515 on the remainder, for a total down payment of $3,265. I contrast, the down payment for the same house financed with conventional loan could run as high as $20,000.

Anyone may apply for an FHA-insured loan, but both the borrowe and the house must qualify.

The VA guarantees loans for eligible veterans, and the husband and wives of those who died while in the service or from service-related disability. The VA guarantees up to 60 percent of th loan or $27,500, whichever is less. Like the FHA, the VA determine the appraised value of the house, though with a VA loan, you ca borrow any amount up to the appraised value.

The Farmers Home Administration offers the only loans mad directly by the government. Families with limited incomes in rur areas can qualify if the house is in a community of less than 10,00 people and is outside of a large metropolitan area; if their income less than $18,000; and if they can prove that they do not qualify for conventional loan.

For more information, write Farmers Home Administration, D partment of Agriculture, Washington, D.C. 20250, or your local offic

New loan instruments

If you think that the escalating cost of housing has squeezed you out the market, take a look at the following new types of mortgages.

The graduated payment mortgage features a monthly obligatic that gradually increases over a negotiated period of time—usually fi to ten years. Though the payments begin lower, they stabilize at higher monthly rate than a standard fixed rate mortgage. Little or equity is built in the first years, a disadvantage if you decide to se early in the mortgage period.

These loans are aimed at young people who can anticipate incom increases that will enable them to meet the escalating payments. Th size of the down payment is about the same or slightly higher than f a conventional loan, but you can qualify with a lower income. As last year, savings and loan associations can write these loans, and th FHA now insures five different types.

The flexible loan insurance program (FLIP) requires that part of th down payment, which is about the same as a conventional loan, placed in a pledged savings account. During the first five years of th mortgage, funds are drawn from this account to supplement the low monthly payments.

The deferred interest mortgage, another graduated program, allov you to pay a lower rate of interest during the first few years and higher rate in the later years of the mortgage. If the house is sold, t borrower must pay back all the interest, often with a prepayme penalty. Both the FLIP and deferred interest loans are very new an not yet widely available.

The variable rate mortgage is most widely available in Californi but its popularity is growing. This instrument features a fluctuatir interest rate that is linked to an economic indicator—usually t lender's cost of obtaining funds for lending. To protect the consum against a sudden and disastrous increase, regulations limit the amou that the interest rate can increase over a given period of time.

To make these loans attractive, lenders offer them without prepa ment penalties and with "assumption" clauses that allow anoth buyer to assume your mortgage should you sell.

Flexible payment mortgages allow young people who can antic pate rising incomes to enter the housing market sooner. They pay on the interest during the first few years; then the mortgage is amortize and the payments go up. This is a valuable option only for tho people who intend to keep their home for several years because equity is built in the lower payment period.

The reverse annuity mortgage is targeted for older people wh have fixed incomes. This new loan allows those who qualify to ta into the equity on their houses. The lender pays them each month ar collects the loan when the house is sold or the owner dies.

LEISURE LIVING LIFESTYLES . . . all

have one thing in common. They are the product of informal living patterns The manner in which these patterns of living are enjoyed can be as varied as our imagination can make them. Here is a potpourri of floor plans which offer the active family a wide range of differing livability features and ways in which to enjoy them. The refreshing, contemporary exteriors seem to announce in a most emphatic fashion the carefree way of life that will surely await the occupants. Since square footages start at 480 and range upward to 3238, there is most assuredly a vacation home here to fit any budget. The wide variety of exteriors will be pleasing, indeed.

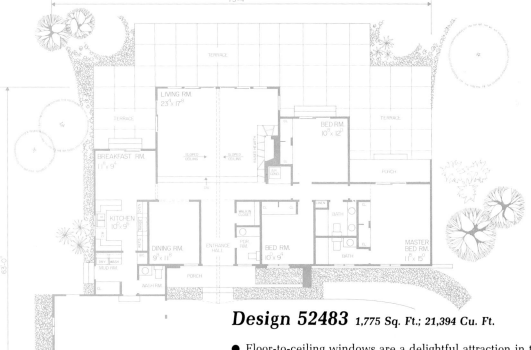

Design 52483 1,775 Sq. Ft.; 21,394 Cu. Ft.

● Floor-to-ceiling windows are a delightful attraction in the living room. Good looking and a way to take advantage of the beautiful outdoor scenery. For more good looks, sloped ceilings and a raised hearth fireplace plus a terrace that runs the length of the house. A formal dining room is convenient to the efficient U-shaped kitchen with a separate breakfast nook. The laundry/mud room will allow immediate clean-up after a day spent fishing or on the beach. Three bedrooms! Including one with a private bath.

Design 52478

1,137 Sq. Ft. - First Floor
257 Sq. Ft. - Second Floor
16,218 Cu. Ft.

● An appealing geometric exterior with a fine floor plan for informal family living. Note the three decks, the big family room, the spacious kitchen, the two fireplaces and the upstairs dormitory.

Design 52480

826 Sq. Ft. - First Floor
533 Sq. Ft. - Second Floor
14,650 Cu. Ft.

● This distinctive contemporary two-story leisure-time home provides excellent living patterns for all. Observe the efficient kitchen, separate laundry, sloped ceilinged living room, two baths and three bedrooms.

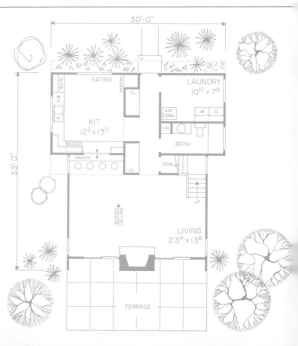

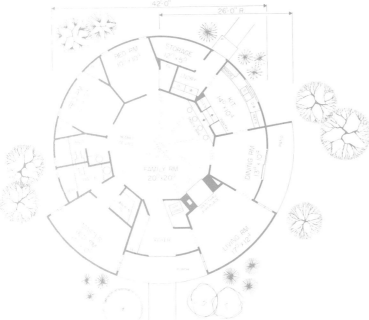

Design 52479
1,547 Sq. Ft.; 14,878 Cu. Ft.

● Here is a unique round house with an equally unique floor plan. The centrally located family room is the focal point around which the various family functions and activities revolve. There is much to study and admire in this plan. For instance, the use of space is most efficient. Notice the strategic location of the kitchen. Don't miss the storage room and laundry. Observe the snack bar, the two-way fireplace, the separate dining room and the two full baths. Fixed glass windows at the beamed ceiling provide natural light from above for the family room.

Three Stacked Levels of Livability

Design 52511

1,043 Sq. Ft. – Main Level; 703 Sq. Ft. – Upper Level
794 Sq. Ft. – Lower Level; 30,528 Cu. Ft.

● Distinctive and newly fashioned, this geometric hillside home offers interesting living patterns. Its interior is as individualistic as its exterior. The main living level is delightfully planned with the efficient kitchen easily serving the snack bar and the dining room. The gathering room has a high ceiling and looks up at the upper level balcony. An angular deck provides the gathering and dining rooms with their outdoor living area. A study with an adjacent full bath, provides the main level with an extra measure of living pattern flexibility. It has its own quiet outdoor balcony. Upstairs, a bunk room, a bedroom and full bath. Also, there is an exciting view through the gathering room windows. On the lower level an optional sleeping facility, the family's all-purpose activities room, a hobby room and another full bath.

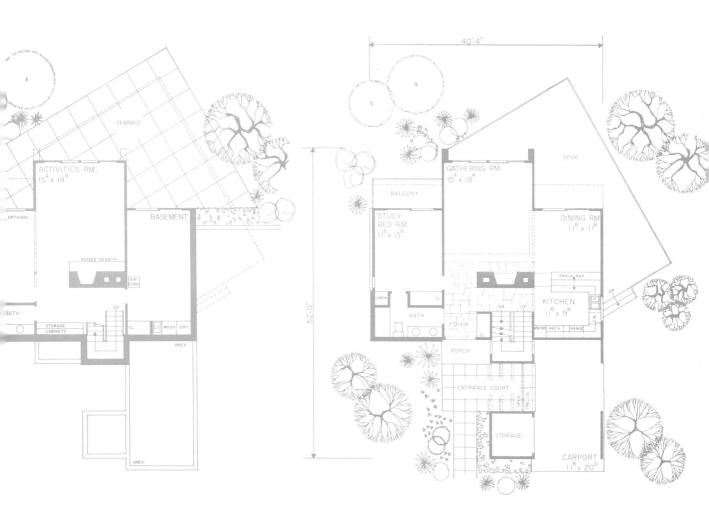

Design 52486 1,124 Sq. Ft. – First Floor; 528 Sq. Ft. – Second Floor; 18,685 Cu. Ft.

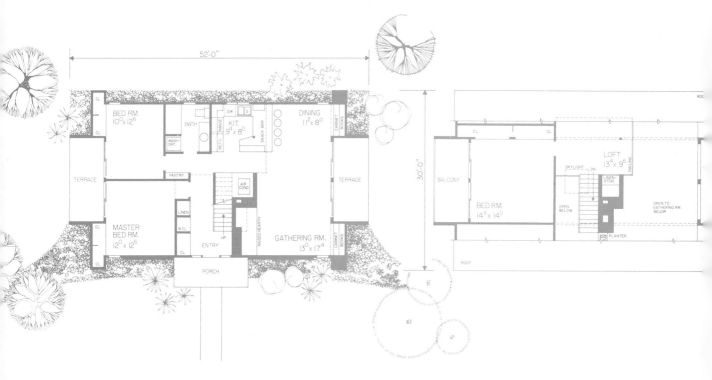

● A two-story vacation home with a distinctive and appealing exterior. Surely the family will welcome the change of pace this retreat represents. It just spells, informality. The living area features a generous 25 foot long gathering room/dining area and a high spacious two-story ceiling. A snack bar and huge counter separate the dining and kitchen areas. Downstairs there are two bedrooms, while upstairs there is a big 14 x 14 foot bedroom plus a loft. A skylight provides plenty of natural light to this area. This compact plan offers fine storage facilities. Even space for a stacked or combination washer and dryer. For indoor-outdoor living there are two terraces and a balcony. This will be a fine family investment which will appreciate in value, as well as memories, as the years pass.

Design 52488 1,113 Sq. Ft. – First Floor; 543 Sq. Ft. – Second Floor; 36,055 Cu. Ft.

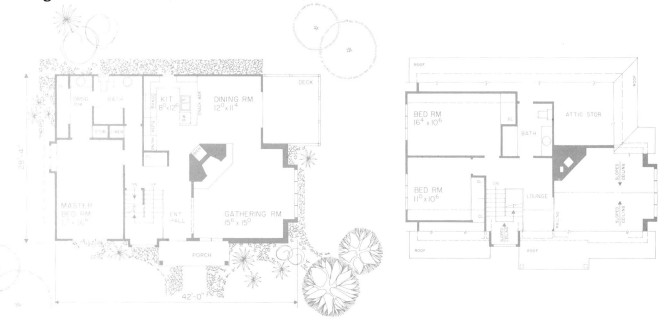

● A cozy cottage for the young at heart! Whether called upon to serve the young active family as a leisure-time retreat at the lake, or the retired couple as a quiet haven in later years, this charming design will perform well. As a year round second home, the up-stairs with its two sizable bedrooms, full bath and lounge area looking down into the gathering room below, will ideally accommodate the younger generation. When called upon to function as a retirement home, the second floor will cater to the visiting family members and friends. Also, it will be available for use as a home office, study, sewing room, music area, the pursuit of hobbies, etc. Of course, as an efficient, economical home for the young, growing family, this design will function well.

13

Design 52470 1,226 Sq. Ft. - Upper Level; 805 Sq. Ft. - Lower Level; 20,210 Cu. Ft.

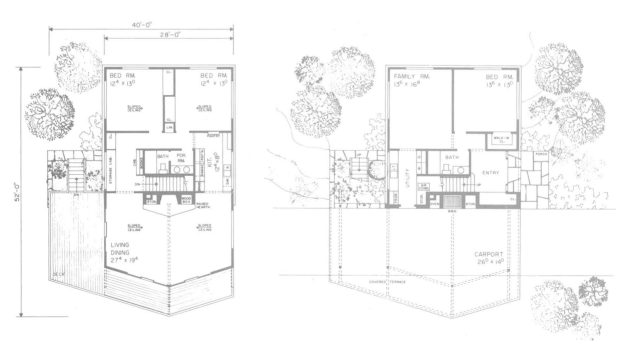

● You will enter this vacation home on the lower level. Here, the main entry routes traffic to the family room and extra bedroom. A full bath is centrally located. Then, up a full flight of stairs to the main living level. There is a feeling of great spaciousness with all those windows and the sloped ceilings. The focal point of the 27 foot living area will be the raised hearth fireplace. Traffic will flow easily to and from the outdoor deck as a result of the three sets of sliding glass doors. The efficient kitchen and good storage facilities will help assure convenient living. On the lower level, below the deck and living area, there is excellent outdoor living potential. This area, may also double as shelter for the car or boat. Don't overlook the outdoor cooking facilities.

Design 51457 640 Sq. Ft. - Upper Level; 640 Sq. Ft. - Lower Level; 11,712 Cu. Ft.

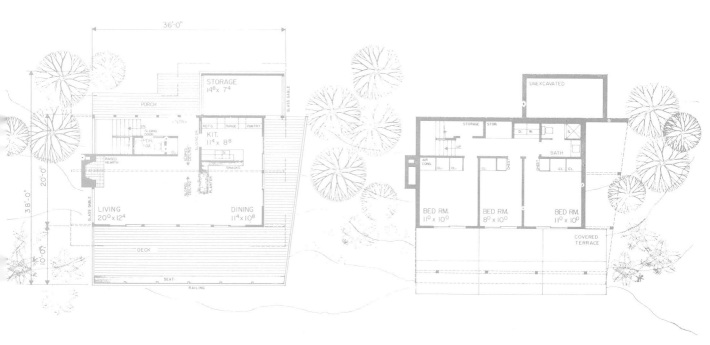

● This hillside vacation home seems to just grow right out of its sloping site. The street view of this design appears to be a one-story. It, therefore, is putting its site to the best possible use. As a result of being able to expose the lower level, the total livable floor area of the house is doubled. This is truly the most practical and economical manner by which to increase livability so dramatically. The upper level is the living level. This is just where you want to be during the day when there is a delightful view to be enjoyed from a high vantage point. For outdoor living there is the big deck which wraps around one side of the house with the covered terrace below sheltered from the weather Dressing rooms are easily accessible when swimming is the primary activity.

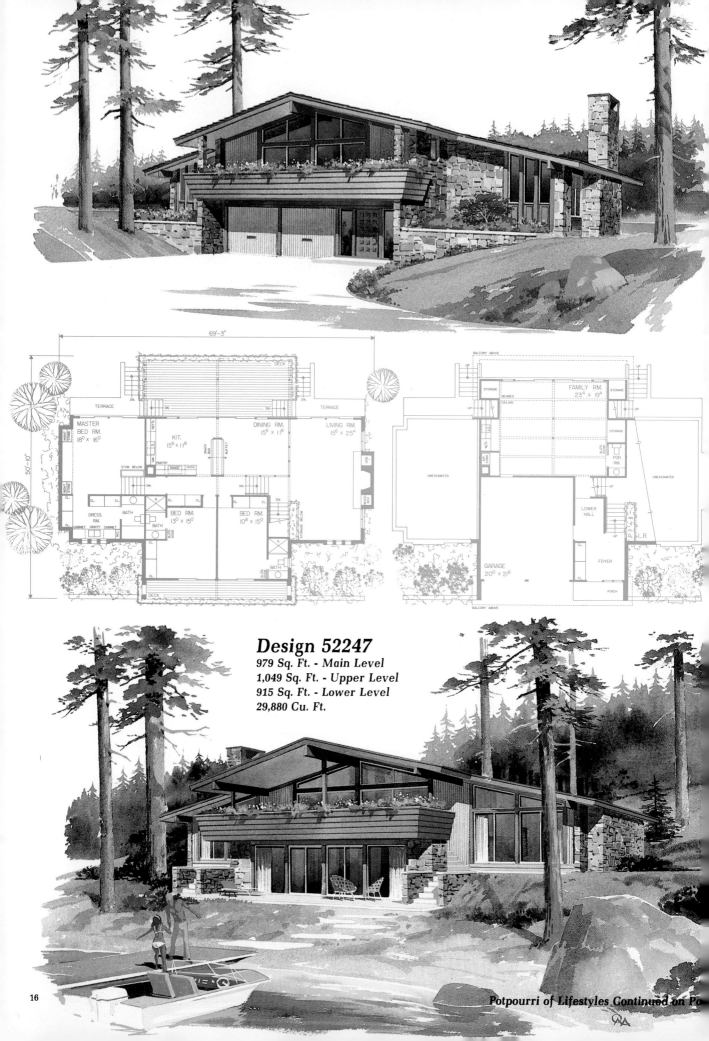

Design 52247

979 Sq. Ft. - Main Level
1,049 Sq. Ft. - Upper Level
915 Sq. Ft. - Lower Level
29,880 Cu. Ft.

Potpourri of Lifestyles Continued on Pa

A-FRAME ADAPTATIONS . . . *have a dramatic flair*

all their own. And little wonder. The soaring roof lines, the expanses of glass, the accompanying decks and balconies, and the uniqueness of their construction all add up to an unmatched measure of distinction. And, inside, the A-frame can be no less impressive. The spaciousness of the living areas are highlighted by the high sloping ceilings and the full measure of cheerful, natural light. A second story, sleeping loft represents a delightful spot to view the fun and goings-on below. Don't miss the truncated versions of this popular vacation home configuration.

Design 52431
1,057 Sq. Ft. - First Floor; 406 Sq. Ft. - Second Floor; 15,230 Cu. Ft.

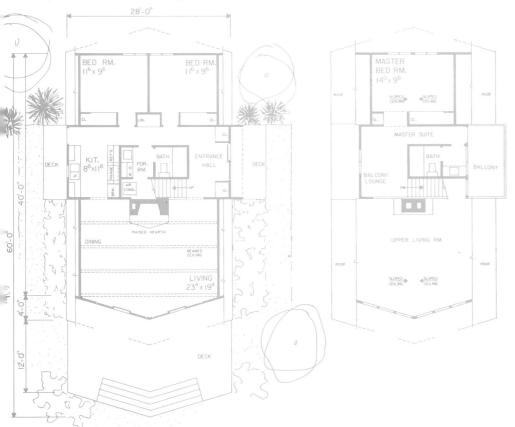

● A favorite everywhere – the A-frame vacation home. Its popularity is easily discernible at first glance. The stately appearance is enhanced by the soaring roof lines and the dramatic glass areas. Inside, the breathtaking beauty of outstanding architectural detailing also is apparent. The high ceiling of the living room slopes and has exposed beams. The second floor master suite is a great feature. Observe the raised hearth fireplace and the outdoor balcony. This outdoor spot certainly will be a quiet perch for sunbathing on a warm afternoon.

Design 52459

1,264 Sq. Ft. – First Floor
556 Sq. Ft. – Second Floor; 18,587 Cu. F

● Dramatic, indeed! The soaring roof projects and heightens the appeal of the slanted glass gable end. The expanse of the roof is broken to provide access to the side deck from the dining room. Above is the balcony of the second floor lounge. This room with its high sloping ceiling looks down into the spacious first floor living room. The master bedroom also has an outdoor balcony. Back downstairs there are loads of features. They include two large bedrooms, a big dining room and a huge living room. Particularly note-worthy is the direct accessibility of the kitchen and mud room/bath from the outdoors. These are truly convenient traffic patterns for the active family. The raised hearth fireplace commands its full share of attention as it rises toward the sloping ceiling.

BED RM.
11⁶ x 11⁰

STOR.

BATH

LIN.

KIT.
8⁸ x 7⁸

REF.

RANGE

S

STOR. STOR. CL. CL.

UP

CL.

STOR.

DINING

24'-0"

32'-0"

16'-0"

LIVING
23⁶ x 15⁸

DN.

DN.

DECK

BALCONY

DORMITORY
15⁰ x 16⁰

ROOF

STOR. CL.

DN.

BALCONY

UPPER LIVING

ROOF

Design 51406

776 Sq. Ft. – First Floor
300 Sq. Ft. – Second Floor; 8,536 Cu. Ft.

● A spacious 23 foot by 15 foot living room is really something to talk about. And when it has a high, vaulted ceiling and a complete wall of windows it is even more noteworthy. Because of the wonderful glass area the livability of the living room seems to spill right out onto the huge wood deck. In addition to the bedroom downstairs, there is the sizable dormitory upstairs for sleeping quite a crew. Sliding glass doors open onto the outdoor balcony from the dormitory. Don't miss the fireplace, the efficient kitchen and the numerous storage facilities. The outside storage units are accessible from just below the roof line and are great for all the recreational equipment. Don't be without the exceptional wood deck. It will make a vital contribution to your outdoor vacation enjoyment.

Design 51436 *1,362 Sq. Ft. – First Floor; 296 Sq. Ft. – Second Floor; 17,998 Cu. Ft.*

● The A-frame and vacation living have practically become synonymous, but don't discount this home as a year 'round one. The idea is catching on and it is a very practical idea at that. Notice how the wings in this version soften the vertical thrust of the "A". And they do more than provide space for two bedrooms and a dining room. They relieve the steep angle of the roof line and add a sense of visual spaciousness to the interior. The second floor can be used as a children's dormitory or as a studio. There's a balcony planned for that floor, too. Note the planter above the fireplace which will be enjoyed from both the living and dining area.

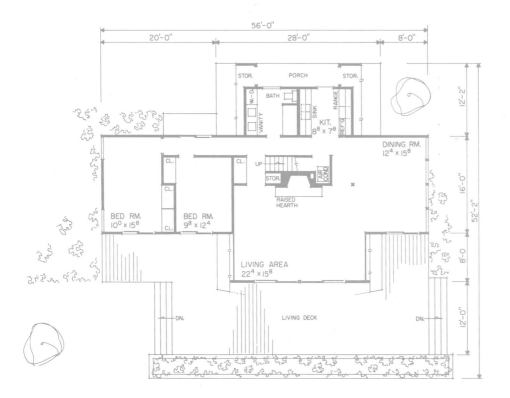
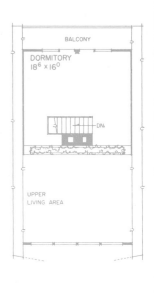

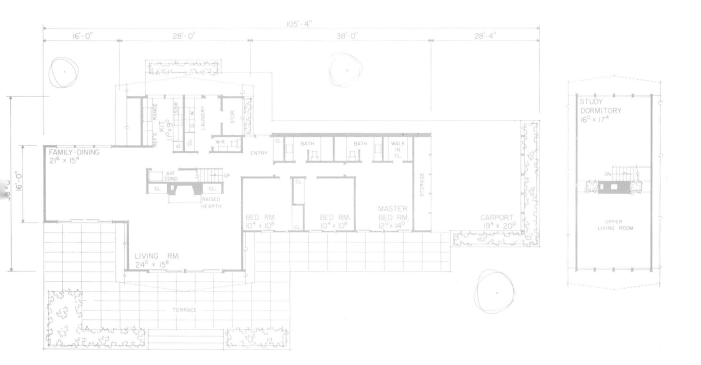

Design 51442 2,012 Sq. Ft. - First Floor; 288 Sq. Ft. - Second Floor; 20,442 Cu. Ft.

● The popularity of the A-frame has made this type of structure a symbol to many people of stylish contemporary living in the carefree manner. Usually associated with the ski lodge or beach cottage, it is a style which responds magnificently to a far more lavish and permanent pattern of living. This A-frame will guarantee its occupants a proud and exciting way of life. Large glass areas and the high ceiling create a spacious atmosphere. The work areas are efficient to cut down those necessary jobs during vacation days. The sleeping area constitutes a wing by itself and features glass sliding doors. Three bedrooms are on the first floor plus a dormitory on the second.

● Perhaps more than any other design in recent years the A-frame has captured the imagination of the prospective vacation home builder. There is a gala air about its shape that fosters a holiday spirit whether the house be a summer retreat or a structure for year 'round living. This particular A-frame offers a lot of living for there are five bedrooms, two baths, an efficient kitchen, a family-dining area and outstanding storage. As in most designs of this type, the living room with its great height and large glass area is extremely dramatic at first sight.

Design 51432 1,512 Sq. Ft. – First Floor; 678 Sq. Ft. – Second Floor; 17,712 Cu. Ft.

Design 51470
1,000 Sq. Ft. – First Floor; 482 Sq. Ft. – Second Floor
243 Sq. Ft. – Loft; 15,718 Cu. Ft.

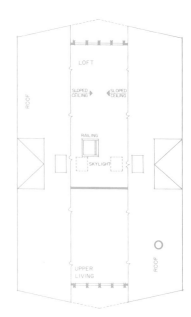

● Three-level, A-frame living can be dramatic and, also, offer your family living patterns that will be a lot of fun all throughout the year. The ceiling of the living room soars upward to an apex of approximately twenty-four feet. Both the second floor and the upper level loft can look down into the living room below. The wall of glass permits a fine view of the outdoors from each of these levels. With all those sleeping facilities even the larg-est of families will have space left over for a few extra friends. Note two baths, efficient kitchen, snack bar and deck which are available to serve your everyday needs. A home to be enjoyed no matter what the occasion.

Design 52466 1,240 Sq. Ft. – First Floor; 815 Sq. Ft. – Second Floor; 19,974 Cu. Ft.

● You will, indeed, find it difficult to improve upon the exterior distinction and the interior livability offered by this truncated A-frame. While the basic dimension of the structure is 24 feet in width, its depth is 48 feet. Cleverly planned within the confines of these dimensions are loads of leisure-time livability with fine provisions made for the fullest enjoyment of the outdoors from within. In addition to the decks for the living and dining rooms, there is the deck servicing the first floor bedrooms. The second floor bedrooms also have an outdoor living area – the balcony. A combination of these features will guarantee enjoyment. Be sure you don't miss such other features as the bunk room, the two full baths, the extra wash room, the mud room and the lounge/balcony of the second floor.

Design 52467 720 Sq. Ft. – First Floor; 483 Sq. Ft. – Second Floor; 10,512 Cu. Ft.

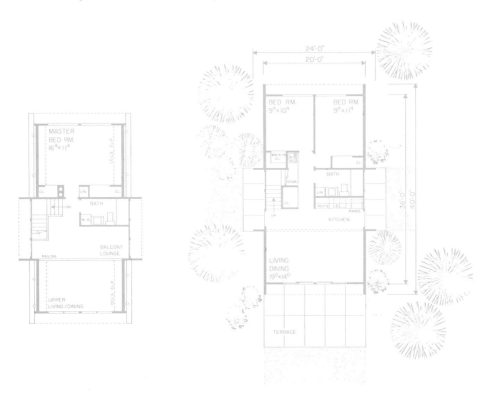

● Here is another dramatic variation of the popular A-frame. The roof modifications result in a structure that is somewhat similar to the configuration of the mansard roof. The utilization of the form with those large glass areas produces a blending of traditional and contemporary design features. The more nearly vertical side walls of this type of a design results in a greater amount of space inside than offered by the usual A-frame. Observe the great amount of livability in this plan. In addition to the two downstairs bedrooms, there is an upstairs master bedroom. Also there is a second full bath and a balcony lounge overlooking the living room. When needed, the lounge area could accommodate a couple of cots for weekend vacationers. Count the storage facilities.

Design 51490
576 Sq. Ft. – First Floor; 362 Sq. Ft. – Second Floor; 6,782 Cu. Ft.

● Wherever situated – in the northern woods, or on the southern coast, these enchanting A-frames will function as perfect retreats. Whether called upon to serve as hunting lodges, ski lodges or summer havens, they will perform admirably. The size of the first floor of each design is identical. However, the layouts are quite different. Which do you prefer Design 51490, above, with a two bedroom second floor or Design 51491, below, with a loft on the second floor?

Design 51491
576 Sq. Ft. – First Floor; 234 Sq. Ft. – Second Floor; 6,757 Cu. Ft.

Design 51494 768 Sq. Ft. – First Floor; 235 Sq. Ft. – Second Floor; 8,191 Cu. Ft.

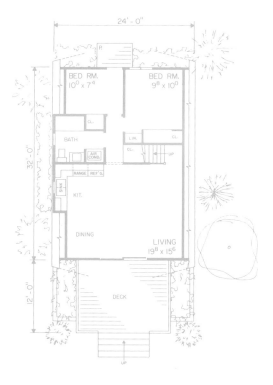

● When you walk out upon your dock with this newly completed A-frame in the background, you will have set the stage for a whole new pattern of living. This efficient second home highlights two bedrooms on the first floor and a dormitory on the second. The high ceiling of the living room is dramatic, indeed.

Design 52471 *1,217 Sq. Ft. – Main Level; 781 Sq. Ft. – Upper Level; 1,240 Sq. Ft. – Lower Level; 29,002 Cu. Ft.*

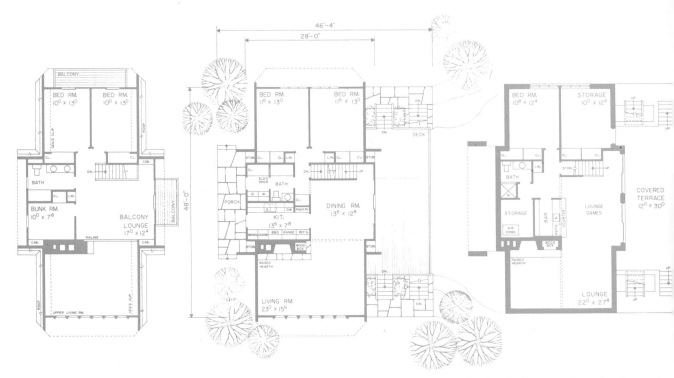

● Whatever the scene – spring, summer, fall or (as above) winter – the dramatic appeal of this modified A-frame will be unsurpassed. And little wonder, too. The exterior with its distinctive roof lines, its outstanding window treatment, its big deck, its covered terrace and its upper level balconies is captivating. The interior with its long list of features is no less unique. Consider, first of all, the various living areas. Each level has its informal lounging area. Then, there are the excellent sleeping facilities highlighted by five bedrooms, plus a bunk room! Each level has a full bath and plenty of storage. For the storing of skiing equipment and boating gear there is even a separate storage room. Don't miss the efficient kitchen and dining room. Eating deck is nearby.

Design 52469 720 Sq. Ft. – First Floor; 483 Sq. Ft. – Second Floor; 10,512 Cu. Ft.

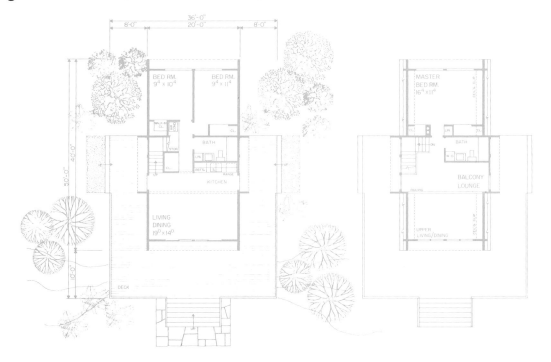

● If yours is a hankering for a truly distinctive second home of modest size with excellent livability and tailored for the moderate building budget, this pleasingly proportioned design may just satisfy your specifications. This 20' x 40' rectangle certainly has its own flair of individuality. Its raised deck and railing add that extra measure of appeal. The projecting roof and sidewalls create a protective recess for the dramatic wall of glass. Such an expanse of glass provides the living-dining area with an abundance of natural light and helps assure a fine awareness of the outdoors. The kitchen is compact and efficient. While there are two bedrooms and full bath downstairs the master bedroom and bath occupy the upper level. The balcony provides extra lounge space.

Design 51476 1,225 Sq. Ft. - Main Level; 560 Sq. Ft. - Upper Level; 905 Sq. Ft. - Lower Level; 29,574 Cu. Ft.

● This colorful A-frame will adapt to its surroundings in a most dramatic manner. The large glass areas and the outdoor decks will permit the fullest enjoyment of the outdoors. The lounges of the lower level and the upper level function with outdoor living areas and will be favorite gathering spots. From the upper level lounge you will look down into the cozy living room. The family dining room will enjoy its own view. It is but a step from the huge deck. There are three bedrooms, 2½ baths and plenty of recreation and storage space.

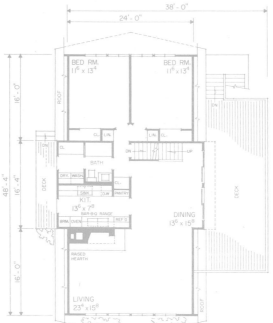

CHALET CHARM . . .

has an image all its own. While it seems to conjure pictures of the rolling Swiss countryside, it has long been a favorite style of many in this country. Whether called upon to function as the family's haven for summer or winter fun, the chalet form will serve its occupants admirably. As seen on the following pages, some chalets have projecting wings for added livability. Others are perfect rectangles with a partial, or a full, upstairs sleeping area. And, of course, some chalets lend themselves to providing three levels of livability. Second story balconies overlooking outdoor decks below complete the picture of leisure living charm and enhance the indoor-outdoor livability that these designs offer.

Design 52456
1,160 Sq. Ft. - First Floor
840 Sq. Ft. - Second Floor; 17,510 Cu. Ft.

● Here's how your Swiss chalet adaptation may look in the winter. Certainly an appealing design whatever the season. A delightful haven for skiers, fishermen and hunters alike. As for sleeping facilities, you'll really be able to pack 'em in. The first floor has two bedrooms plus a room which will take a double bunk. Across the hall is the compartment bath. A disappearing stair unit leads to the children's bunk room. The placement of single bunks or cots will permit the sleeping of three or four more. A bath with stall shower is nearby. The master bedroom suite is complete with walk-in closet, dressing room and private bath and opens onto the balcony. There is plenty of space in the L-shaped living-dining area with wood box and fireplace to accommodate the whole gang.

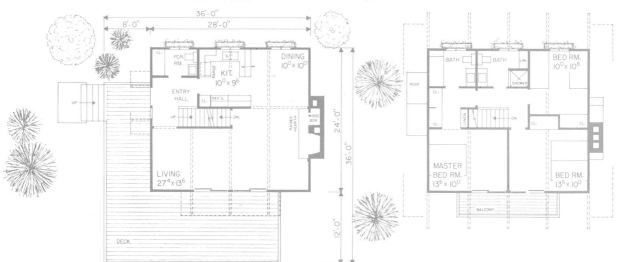

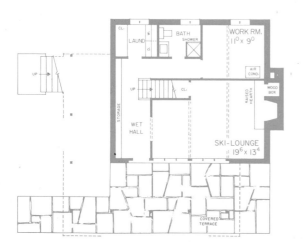

Design 52429

672 Sq. Ft. – Main Level; 672 Sq. Ft. – Upper Level
672 Sq. Ft. – Lower Level; 19,152 Cu. Ft.

● A ski lodge with a Swiss chalet character. If you
are a skier, you know that all the fun is not restricted to schussing the slopes. A great portion of the
pleasure is found in the living accommodations and
the pursuant merriment fostered by good fellowship.
As for the specific features which will surely
contribute to everyone's off-the-slopes fun consider:
the outdoor deck, balcony and covered terrace; the
ski lounge; the two fireplaces; and the huge L-
shaped living and dining room area. The three bedrooms are of good size and with bunk beds will
sleep quite a crew. Note the wet hall for skis, the all
important work room and the laundry.

Design 52430 1,238 Sq. Ft. – First Floor; 648 Sq. Ft. – Second Floor; 18,743 Cu. Ft.

Another Swiss chalet adaptation which will serve its occupants admirably during the four seasons of the year. The sun-drenched balcony and the terrace will be enjoyed as much by the skiers in the winter as by the swimmers in the summer. All the var-ious areas are equally outstanding. For sleeping, there are four big bedrooms. They are supported by two full baths – one has both tub and stall shower. For relaxation, there is the big living room. It has a fireplace and a large glass area to preserve the view. For eating, there is the U-shaped kitchen and its adja-cent dining area. Don't miss beamed ceilings of first floor, nor sloping ceil-ings of second floor. Note the position-ing of the lake bath adjacent to the kitchen entrance. Truly a strategic and convenient location.

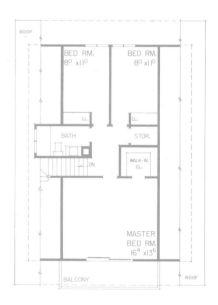

Design 51482 *1,008 Sq. Ft. – First Floor; 637 Sq. Ft. – Second Floor; 16,657 Cu. Ft.*

● Here's a chalet right from the pages of the travel folders. Whether the setting reflects the majestic beauty of a winter scene, or the tranquil splendor of a summer landscape, this design will serve its occupants well. In addition to the big bedrooms on the first floor, there are three more upstairs. The large master bedroom has a balcony which looks down into the lower wood deck. There are two full baths. The first floor bath is directly accessible from the outdoors. Note snack bar and pantry of the kitchen. Laundry area is adjacent to side door.

Design 51473 *672 Sq. Ft. – First Floor; 234 Sq. Ft. – Second Floor; 9,677 Cu. Ft.*

● You won't find many leisure-time designs with more charm than this compact, efficient and low cost home. The moderately pitched, wide-overhanging roof and the strikingly simple glass areas result in a very positive and pleasing identity. Three pairs of sliding glass doors open from the wood deck into the cheerfully lighted living area with its high sloping ceiling. A corner of this generous living area will be more than adequate for the preparation of meals. Across the room is the appealing prefabricated fireplace. Note storage units.

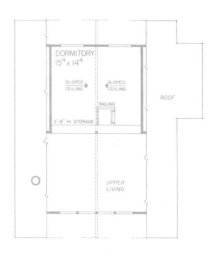

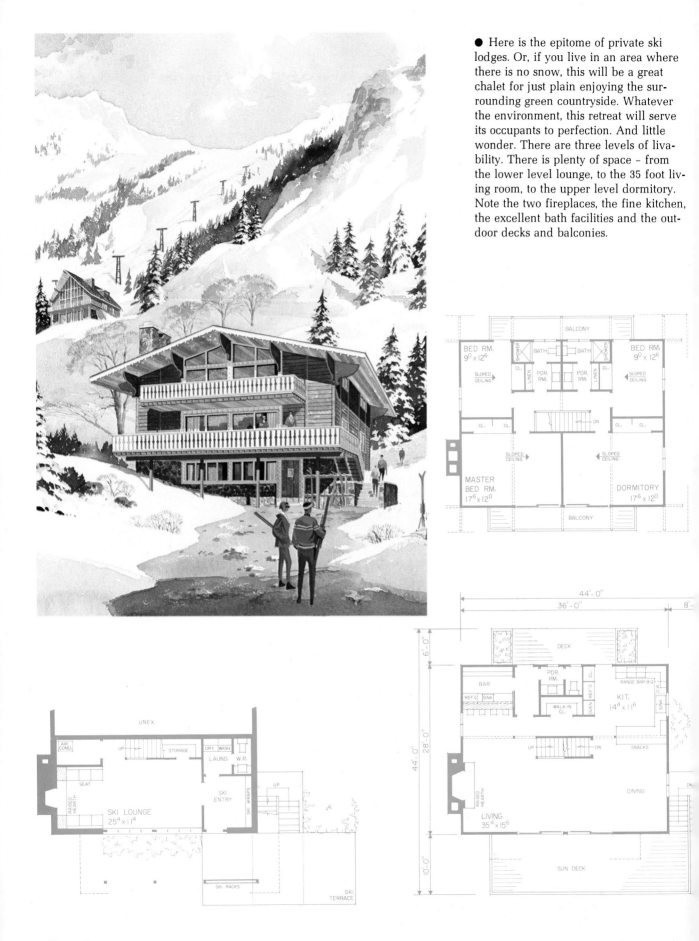

● Here is the epitome of private ski lodges. Or, if you live in an area where there is no snow, this will be a great chalet for just plain enjoying the surrounding green countryside. Whatever the environment, this retreat will serve its occupants to perfection. And little wonder. There are three levels of livability. There is plenty of space – from the lower level lounge, to the 35 foot living room, to the upper level dormitory. Note the two fireplaces, the fine kitchen, the excellent bath facilities and the outdoor decks and balconies.

Design 51474 1,008 Sq. Ft. – Main Level; 1,008 Sq. Ft. – Upper Level; 594 Sq. Ft. – Lower Level; 23,802 Cu. Ft.

Design 51475 *1,120 Sq. Ft. – Main Level; 522 Sq. Ft. – Upper Level; 616 Sq. Ft. – Lower Level; 24,406 Cu. Ft.*

● Skiers take notice! This vacation home tells an exciting story of activity – and people. Whether you build this design to function as your ski lodge, or to serve your family and friends during the summer months, it will perform ideally. It would take little imagination to envision this second home overlooking your lakeshore site with the grown-ups sunning themselves on the deck while the children play on the terrace. Whatever the season or the location, visualize how your family will enjoy the many hours spent in this delightful chalet adaptation.

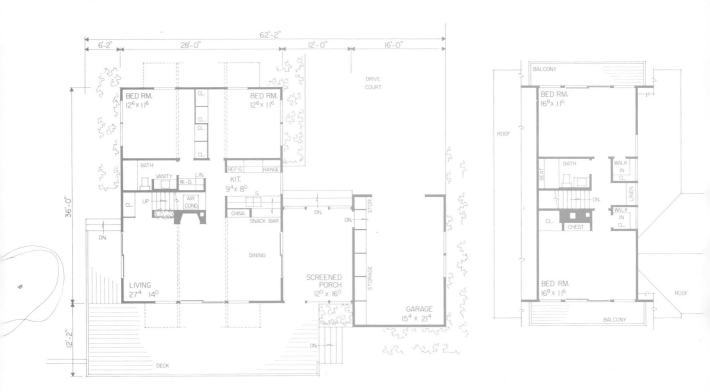

Design 51422 *1,008 Sq. Ft. – First Floor; 624 Sq. Ft. – Second Floor; 15,044 Cu. Ft.*

● The chalet influence takes over on this design. If you have a big family, the four bedrooms of this vacation home will force you to take the second look. Notice the balcony off of each bedroom on the second floor and the fact that each bedroom has a walk-in closet. The first floor highlights many features highly desirable in the year-round home. Among these are the open-stairway with planter, the fireplace, the china cabinet and snack bar, the bathroom vanity and the efficient kitchen which will be free of unnecessary thru traffic. Outdoor living will be enjoyed on the two outdoor balconies, the deck and even the screened-in porch between house and garage.

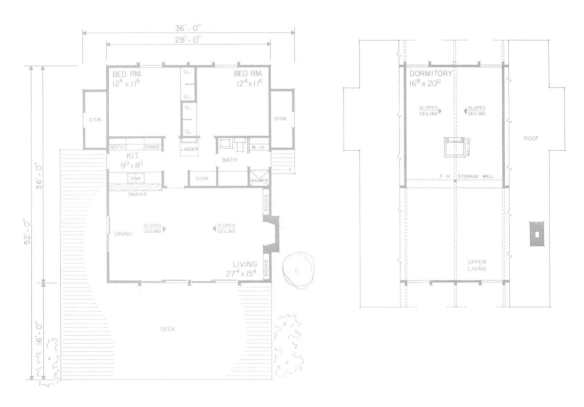

Design 51472 1,008 Sq. Ft. – First Floor; 546 Sq. Ft. – Second Floor; 13,608 Cu. Ft.

● Wherever perched, this smart leisure-time home will surely make your visits memorable ones. The large living area with its sloped ceiling, dramatic expanses of glass and attractive fireplace will certainly offer the proper atmosphere for quiet relaxation. Keeping house will be no chore for the weekend homemaker. The kitchen is compact and efficient. There is plenty of storage space for all the necessary recreational equipment. There is a full bath and even a stall shower accessible from the outside for use by the swimmers. A ladder leads to the second floor sloped ceiling dormitory which overlooks the living/dining area. Ideal for the younger generation.

● It will not make any difference where you locate this chalet-type second home. The atmosphere it creates will be one for true leisure living. To guarantee sheer enjoyment you wouldn't even have to be situated close to the water. And little wonder with such an array of features as: the big deck, the fine porch and the two balconies. For complete livability there are four bedrooms, two full baths, an outstanding U-shaped kitchen, a large living area with a raised hearth fireplace and a super-abundance of closet and storage facilities. Of particular interest is the direct access from outdoors to the first floor bath with its stall shower.

Design 52412
1,120 Sq. Ft. – First Floor
664 Sq. Ft. – Second Floor
18,680 Cu. Ft.

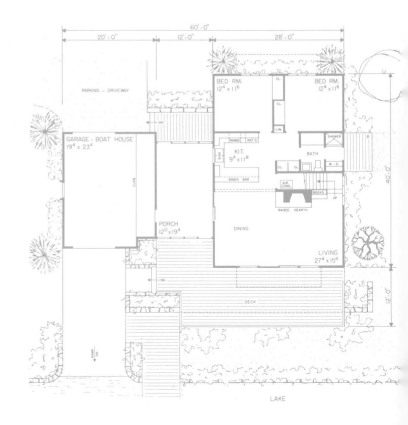

GEOMETRIC SHAPES . . .

offer interesting and exciting configurations which seem to establish the desired ambience for fun-filled, informal, vacation home living. And in many cases, the room relationships and how they function with the outdoors, are unique, indeed. As is so often the case, preserving a view of the surrounding countryside and exploiting it to the fullest, is an objective to be achieved. Locating glass areas in a strategic fashion can assure unbounded enjoyment of outdoor vistas. These designs, whatever their shapes, attain their objective admirably. Be sure to contrast the varying living patterns these designs offer for consideration. Varying sizes will appeal to a great deal of building budgets.

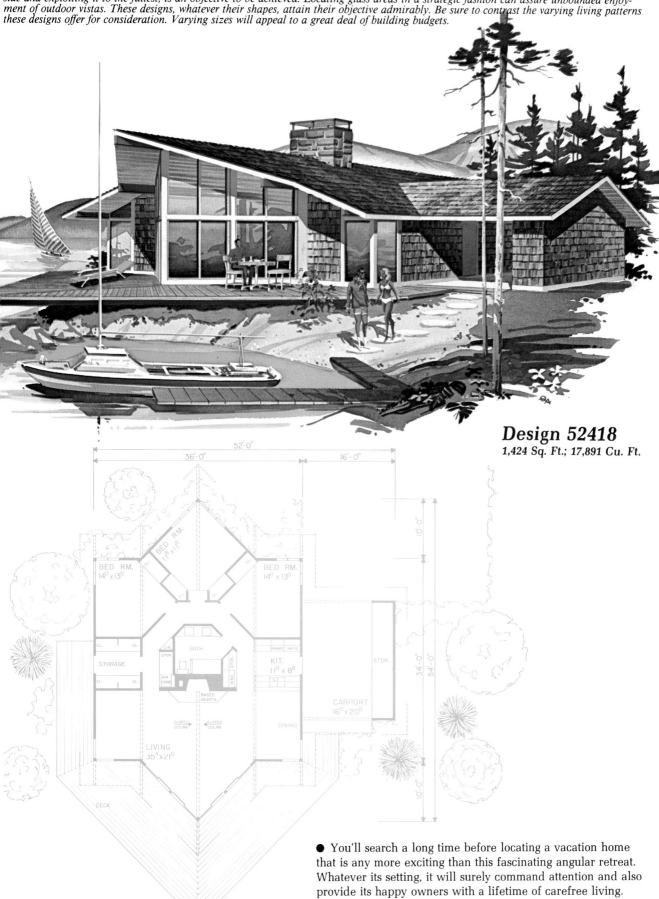

Design 52418
1,424 Sq. Ft.; 17,891 Cu. Ft.

● You'll search a long time before locating a vacation home that is any more exciting than this fascinating angular retreat. Whatever its setting, it will surely command attention and also provide its happy owners with a lifetime of carefree living. The soaring roof lines, the cedar shakes, the appealing glass areas and the sloping, beamed ceilings are features.

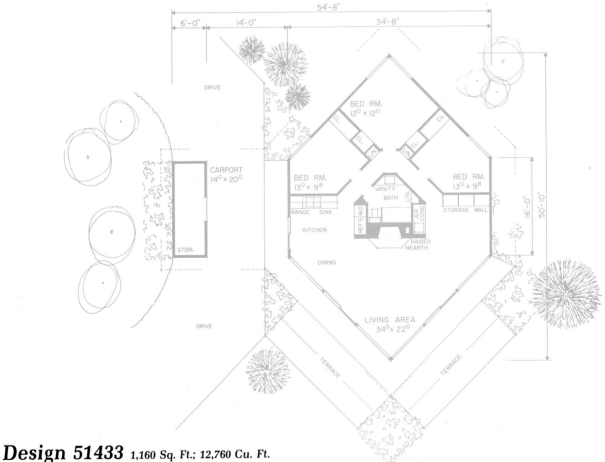

Design 51433 1,160 Sq. Ft.; 12,760 Cu. Ft.

● This hexagonal vacation, or leisure-time, home surely will prove to be a delightful haven away from the conventions of everyday living. Like a breath of fresh air, its uniqueness will make the hours spent in and around this second home memorable ones, in-deed. The floor plan, in spite of its shape, reflects a wise and economical use of space. The spacious interior features a raised hearth fireplace, abundant storage facilities, a bathroom vanity and a combination washer-dryer space. Then, there is the attached car-port and its bulk storage area for recreational and garden equipment. The wide, overhanging roof provides for protection from the rays of the hot summer sun. This will be a great house from which to enjoy the beauty of the countryside.

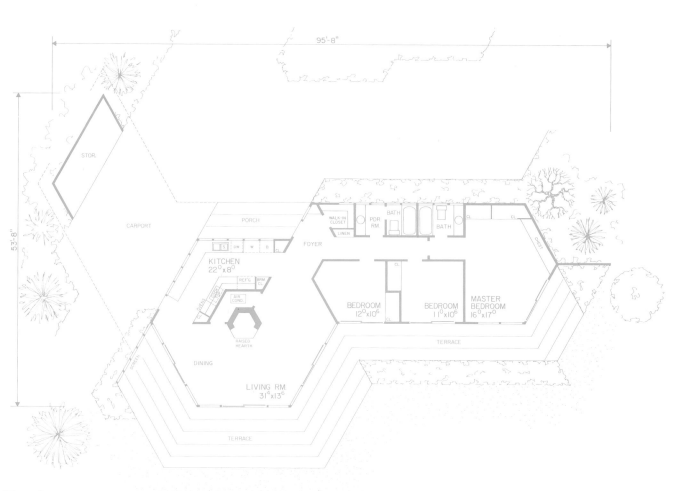

Floor plan labels: 95'-8", 53'-8", STOR., CARPORT, PORCH, WALK-IN CLOSET, LINEN, PDR RM, BATH, BATH, FOYER, KITCHEN 22⁰x8⁰, REF'G, BRM CL, AIR COND., RAISED HEARTH, BEDROOM 12⁰x10⁶, BEDROOM 11⁰x10⁶, MASTER BEDROOM 16⁰x17⁰, TERRACE, DINING, SCREEN, LIVING RM 31'⁴x13⁶, TERRACE

Design 51453 1,476 Sq. Ft.; 13,934 Cu. Ft.

● An exciting design, unusual in character, yet fun to live in. This frame home with its vertical siding and large glass areas has as its dramatic focal point a hexagonal living area which gives way to interesting angles. The large living area features sliding glass doors through which traffic may pass to the terrace stretching across the entire length of the house. The wide overhanging roof projects over the terrace and results in a large covered area outside the sliding doors of the master bedroom. The sloping ceilings converge above the unique open fireplace with its copper hood. The drive approach and the angles of the covered front entrance make this an eye-catching design. Surely an extraordinary design for a new lease on living for summer or winter fun.

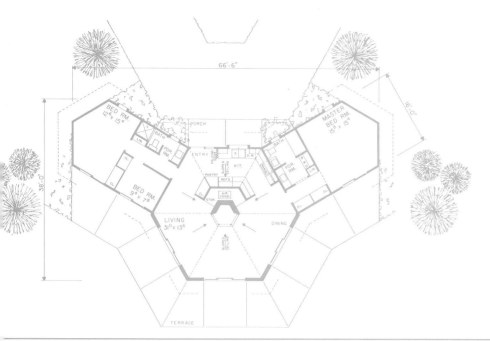

Design 52461
1,400 Sq. Ft.; 13,742 Cu. Ft.

● If you have the urge to make your vacation home one that has a distinctive flair of individuality, you should give consideration to the three designs illustrated here. Not only will you love the unique exterior appeal of your new home; but, also, the exceptional living patterns offered by the interior. The basic living area is a hexagon. To this space conscious geometric shape is added the sleeping wings with baths. The center of the living area has as its focal point a dramatic fireplace.

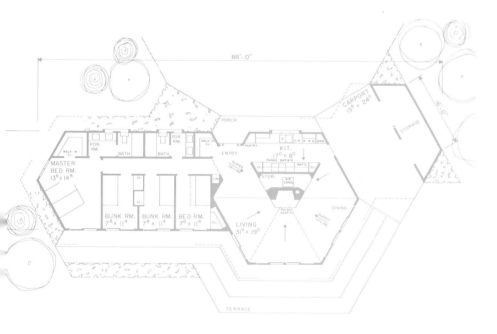

Design 52458
1,406 Sq. Ft.; 14,108 Cu. Ft.

● The six-sided living unit of each design is highlighted by sloping ceilings and an abundance of glass to assure a glorious feeling of spaciousness. The homemaker's center is efficient and will be a delight in which to prepare and serve meals. The design at left highlights a large master bedroom and three bunk rooms. The bath facilities are compartmented and feature twin lavatories. To service the family's storage needs there are two walk-in closets, utility unit and a bulk storage unit.

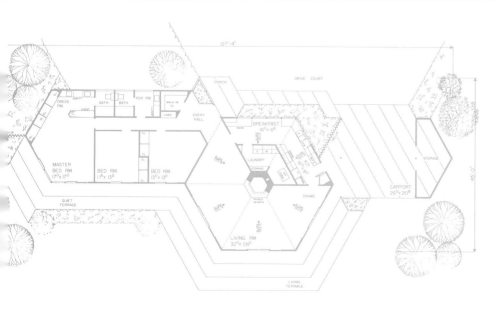

Design 52468
2,140 Sq. Ft.; 20,409 Cu. Ft.

● A major identifying characteristic of these three designs is the roof structure. The chimneys are an interesting design feature. Of significance are the indoor-outdoor relationships. Sliding glass doors put the sleeping and living areas but a step from the outdoor terraces. A comparison of sizes of these three designs is interesting. Which design satisfies your family's requirements best? Which best satisfies the budget?

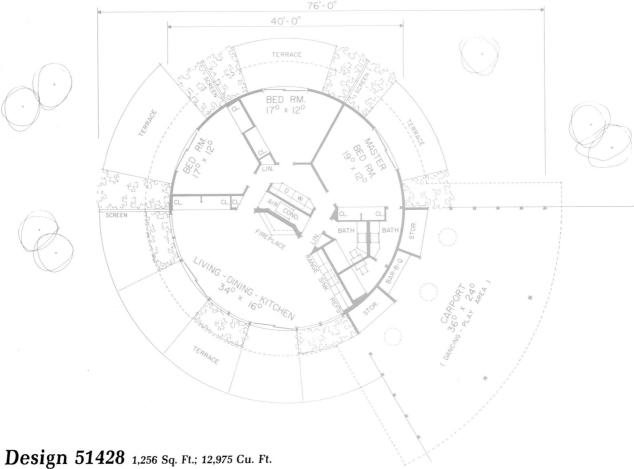

Design 51428 1,256 Sq. Ft.; 12,975 Cu. Ft.

● A round house is ideal for a light-hearted atmosphere, and what better spot for the light-in-heart than a vacation home? Terraces surround its circumference, accessible from each portion of the living and sleeping areas through sliding glass doors. The living area with its strip kitchen and dining space flares out from the dramatic fireplace. For economy, all the plumbing has been concentrated in one segment of the circle. The master bath and the second bath are located back-to-back. Note huge carport with barbecue and the privacy fences. This would be a great area for family outdoor activities when that never wanted inclement weather arrives.

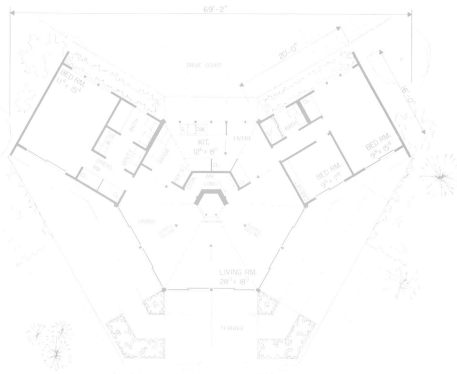

Design 51404 *1,336 Sq. Ft.; 12,230 Cu. Ft.*

● Here is an exciting design, unusual in character, yet fun to live in. This design with its frame exterior and large glass areas has as its dramatic focal point a hexagonal living area which gives way to interesting angles. The spacious living area features sliding glass doors through which traffic may pass to the terraces stretching across the entire length of the house. The wide overhanging roofs project over the terraces, thus providing partial protection from the weather. The sloping ceilings converge above the unique open fireplace. The sleeping areas are located in each wing from the hexagonal center. Three bedrooms in all to serve the family.

Design 52439 1,312 Sq. Ft.; 17,673 Cu. Ft.

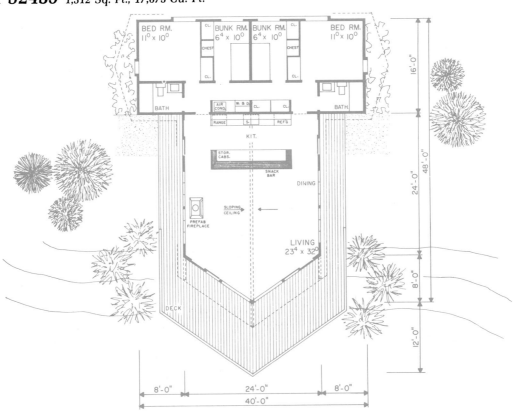

● A wonderfully organized plan with an exterior that will surely command the attention of each and every passerby. And what will catch the eye? Certainly the roof lines and the pointed glass gable end wall will be noticed immediately. The delightful deck will be quickly noticed, too. Inside a visitor will be thrilled by the spaciousness of the huge living room. The ceilings slope upward to the exposed ridge beam. A free-standing fireplace will make its contribution to a cheerful atmosphere. The kitchen is separated from the living area by a three foot high snack bar with cupboards below servicing the kitchen. What could improve upon the sleeping zone when it has two bedrooms, two bunk rooms, two full baths, two built-in chests and fine closet space?

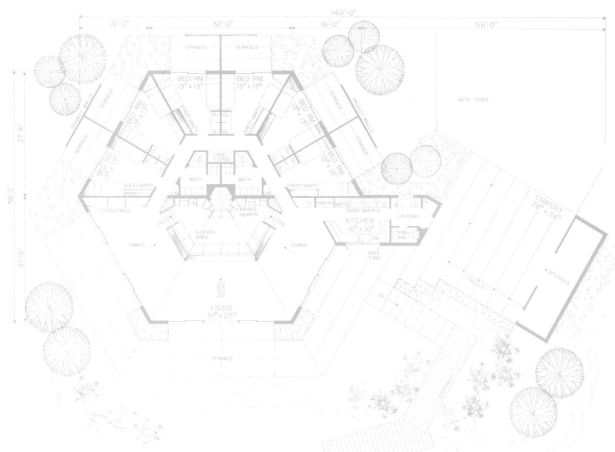

Design 51443 2,928 Sq. Ft.; 31,393 Cu. Ft.

● Is yours a big family? If so, you'll find the living and sleeping accommodations offered by this interesting hexagon exceptional, indeed. The spacious living area features plenty of glass and sliding doors which permit maximum enjoyment of the outdoors from within. A sunken area with built-in furniture in front of the raised hearth fireplace will be the favorite gathering spot. The sleeping area consists of six bedrooms. Built-in bunks would permit the sleeping of as many as 24 persons. Observe how each bed-room functions through sliding glass doors with its own outdoor terrace. Note the closet facilities and the built-in chest-vanity in each room. Two centrally located baths highlight twin lavatories and stall showers. Plumbing facilities are economically grouped.

Design 51460 1,035 Sq. Ft. – Upper Level; 1,067 Sq. Ft. – Lower Level; 21,125 Cu. Ft.

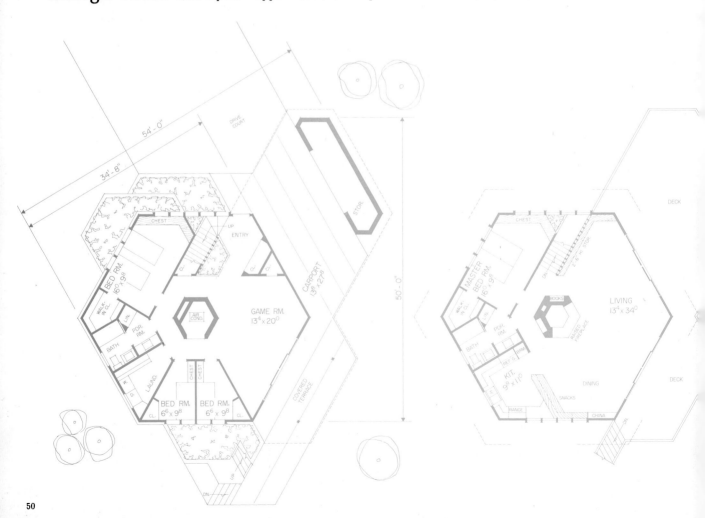

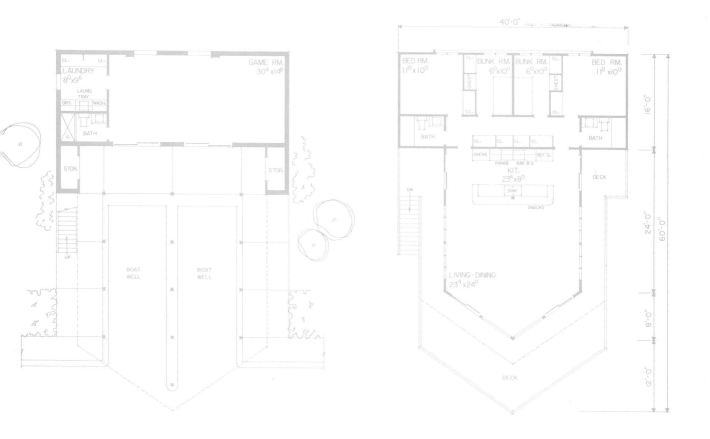

Design 51480 1,312 Sq. Ft. – Upper Level; 640 Sq. Ft. – Lower Level; 20,972 Cu. Ft.

51

Design 52436 *1,094 Sq. Ft.; 13,551 Cu. Ft.*

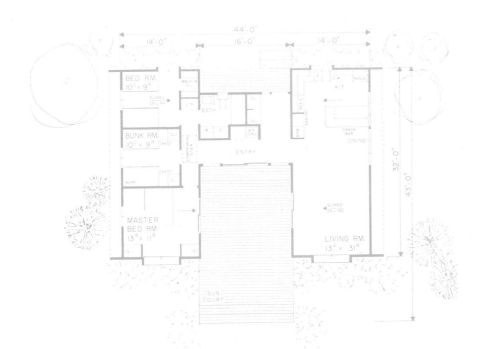

● The unique exterior of this design is only the beginning of the list of many features that will delight you about this vacation home. And unique it certainly is! Study the contrast of window and wall space. Note the roof pitch. Upon entrance through the sun court, one will be greeted at the front entry. To one side is the living area consisting of kitchen, dining and living area. The kitchen is convenient and has the feature of a snack bar for very informal dining. This whole living area along with the bedroom wing has sloping ceilings. The master bedroom, bunk room and another bedroom are located in the bedroom wing. A full bath with washer and dryer are in the center of the plan. This home will be a welcomed addition for any leisure-time location.

Design 52413 1,600 Sq. Ft.; 16,608 Cu. Ft.

● Vacation living by its very nature represents a departure from the usual year 'round daily routine. If there is a vacation home in your future, you can, and should, choose one which represents a departure from the year 'round homestead. The design on this page is illustrative of the degree to which you can make your second home distinctive. This design will admirably satisfy your flair for good taste and individuality. As you and your family review this plan, you'll have fun discussing your family's individual living patterns and how you'd want your new vacation home to cater to them. Consider the indoor-outdoor informal living areas. Also important are the various room locations and their orientation with respect to the enjoyment of views of the outdoor surroundings.

Design 51431 1,632 Sq. Ft.; 17,136 Cu. Ft.

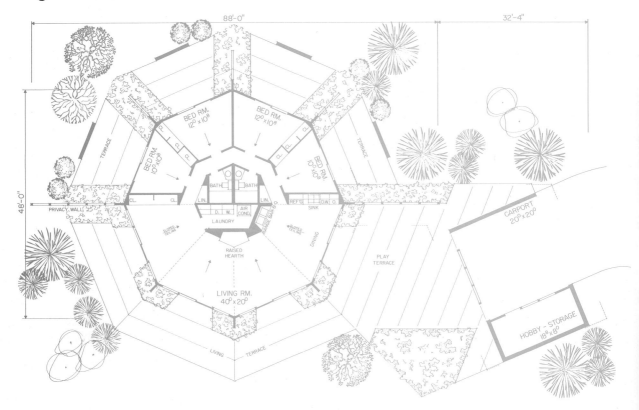

Design 51463
1,456 Sq. Ft.; 14,928 Cu. Ft.

● A leisure-time home can represent a delightful departure from your year 'round home. Your choice of something new and different in the way of exterior design will be refreshing. The selection of a unique, yet practical, floor plan will result in living patterns which will give your family a complete change of pace. This contemporary home highlights a spacious, center living core which is flanked by low-slung, flat-roofed sleeping wings. The overall impact of the exterior is one of pure distinction. Inside, there is an atmosphere of cheerfulness fostered by the open planning, the walls of glass, the sloping ceilings and the fireplace. The children have their own sleeping area, while the parents have theirs. Note the two baths, mud room and decks.

Design 52417 1,520 Sq. Ft.; 19,952 Cu. Ft.

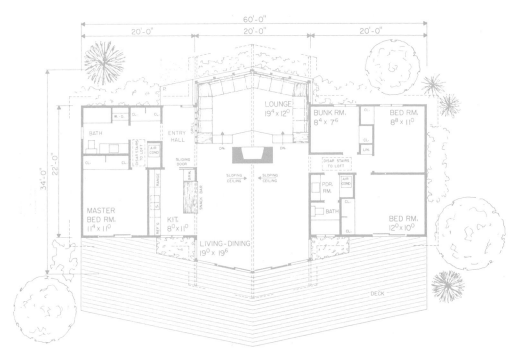

● Have you ever seen a vacation home design that is anything quite like this one? Probably not. The picturesque exterior is dominated by a projecting gable with its wide overhanging roof acting as a dramatic sun visor for the wonderfully large glass area below.

Effectively balancing this 20 foot center section are two 20 foot wings. Inside, and below the high, sloping, beamed ceiling is the huge living area. In addition to the living-dining area, there is the spacious sunken lounge. This pleasant area has a built-in seat-

ing arrangement and a cozy fireplace. The kitchen is efficient and handy to the snack bar and dining area. The parents' and children's sleeping areas are separated and each has a full bath The large deck is accessible from sliding glass doors.

ONE-STORY HOLIDAY HOMES . . .

offer the optimum in vacation living simplicity and convenience. However, as the designs on the following pages illustrate, such livability can represent a delightful break from one's every-day, back home, routine. Whatever the size of your second home budget, you'll find that each of these appealing designs offer you open living areas with dual-use potential and a fine feeling of spaciousness. Kitchen/nook areas are complete and efficient as are bath and storage facilities. Fireplaces, sloping ceilings, decks, terraces, and carports are features worthy of note. Sleeping facilities are wide-ranging; from one bedroom to accommodations for many.

Design 52457 1,288 Sq. Ft.; 13,730 Cu. Ft.

● Leisure living will indeed be graciously experienced in this hip-roofed second home. Except for the clipped corner, it is a perfect square measuring 36 x 36 feet. The 23 foot square living room enjoys a great view of the surrounding environment by virtue of the expanses of glass. The wide overhanging roof affords protection from the sun. The "open planning" adds to the spaciousness of the interior. The focal point is the raised hearth fireplace. The three bedrooms are served by two full baths which are also accessible to other areas. The kitchen, looking out upon the water, will be a delight in which to work. Observe the carport, the big bulk storage room and the dressing room with its stall shower. What great planning for a leisure-time second home.

Design 52416
1,051 Sq. Ft.; 12,087 Cu. Ft.

● As viewed from the lake, the adjoining ski slope or down the path apiece, the front exterior of this design is highlighted by the dramatic glass gable. The wide overhanging roof and the masses of masonry add their note of distinction to this three bedroom second home. All the elements are present to permit year 'round living. The raised hearth fireplace, along with the wall of glass sliding doors, makes the living area an outstanding one. The kitchen has all the conveniences of home.

Design 51417
976 Sq. Ft.; 8,618 Cu. Ft.

● The forward look of this design results from the folded-plate roof. It rests on sturdy posts and beams and extends over the big outdoor living deck. The deck connects the living room-kitchen with two bedrooms and a bath. The deck affords access to the house from both the front and rear, and has two storage walls. Both enclosed areas have large glass walls. Come rain, or come shine, this is a second home you'll have fun living in. It is also one that will be long remembered.

Design 52428
1,120 Sq. Ft.; 12,463 Cu. Ft.

● This delightfully different vacation home will provide you with years of complete satisfaction. Your investment will deliver to you and your family a constant pride of ownership. As you sit upon the wood deck enjoying the view, at your back will be a distinctive exterior with an equally unique interior. A front-to-rear living area separates the children's bedrooms from the parents' master bedroom. There are two full baths – one with a tub, the other with a stall shower. The living area with its glass gable, high sloping ceiling, free-standing fireplace and large built-in dining surface, is exciting, indeed. Notice the skylite in the children's bathroom.

Design 51412
1,138 Sq. Ft.; 9,855 Cu. Ft.

● If you have a vacationland view you wish to preserve and enjoy to the fullest from your living area, here's a design worthy of your consideration. Sloping ceilings and all that glass foster a fine feeling of spaciousness. Should your future plans call for complete retirement to your leisure-time retreat, this design will function admirably as a year 'round home. Study the various features of the plan carefully. Notice the wonderful efficiency of the kitchen.

Design 52405
874 Sq. Ft.; 8,740 Cu. Ft.

● Your sloping lakeside site surely will be a much talked about show place with this dramatic contemporary weekend home on it. The shed roof with its exposed rafters projects out over the outdoor balcony. While so doing, the overhang acts as a visor for that fine wall of glass panels. And this plan won't just be a weekend retreat, either. It has all the features to allow it to serve well as a year 'round second home.

Design 51440
1,248 Sq. Ft.; 10,807 Cu. Ft.

● Here is a smart vacation home which derives its appeal from the simplicity of its exterior and the originality of its interior. The raised, partially covered decks provide outdoor living areas adjacent to the spacious, informal indoor living area. The focal point of course will be the open fireplace around which a free flow of activities will take place. Projecting from this sloped ceiling living area are two bedroom wings. Each wing features two bedrooms and a full bath with a stall shower. Cabinets below the lavatory and the two linen closets provide additional storage areas.

Design 52462

1,256 Sq. Ft.; 12,003 Cu. Ft.

● Whether you choose the living room deck or the bedroom deck for relaxation, you'll experience a delightful air of contentment. This second home has all the features you and your family would want to help guarantee year 'round enjoyment. Consider the spacious living area with its sloping ceiling and wall of glass. Note the bedroom wing with all those bath and storage facilities. Observe the storage room with its stall shower and washer-dryer. Don't miss snack bar, fireplace, efficient kitchen and sliding glass doors.

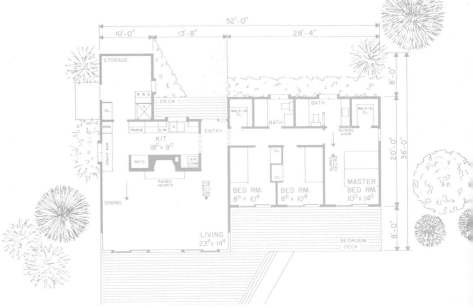

Design 52400

1,526 Sq. Ft.; 14,135 Cu. Ft.

● Here is a smart looking leisure-time home that permits all the living and sleeping areas to have an outdoor view. All those windows also foster a glorious atmosphere of indoor spaciousness. There are two baths plus an extra wash room. Note its similarity in floor plans to Design 52462 at the top of the page. Which do you like the best? It is interesting to observe the dissimilarity of the exteriors with similar basic floor plans. Don't overlook the size differential of the two designs.

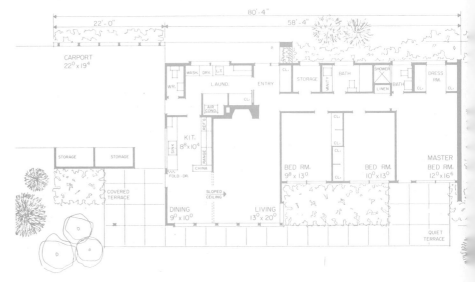

Design 52460
992 Sq. Ft.; 8,778 Cu. Ft.

● Here is a basic rectangle of 24 feet by 36 feet – 864 square feet without storage room – which will be economical to build. With its low-pitched, wide overhanging roof and its glass gable above the two sliding glass door units this is a most attractive design. The sloping ceilings add a dimension of spaciousness to the well-planned interior. The construction of the storage room adds vital convenient living features – an abundance of bulk storage space. The carport will be a great location for off season boat storage.

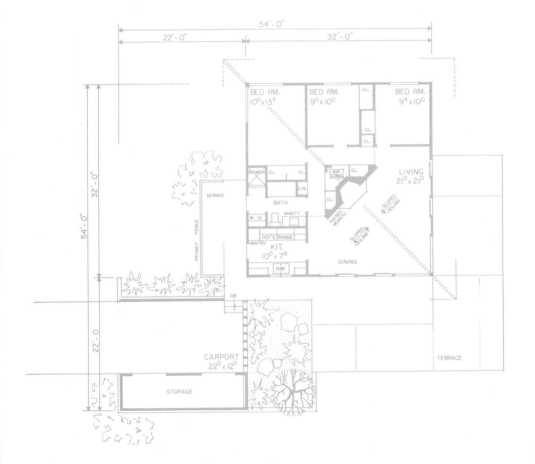

Design 51469
1,024 Sq. Ft.; 10,342 Cu. Ft.

● A new lease on living will be your reward when you and your family begin to enjoy the informal living patterns offered by this economically built retreat. The house itself is a perfect, 32 foot square. The living area with all that glass, sloping ceilings and attractive raised hearth fireplace will maintain an airy and cheerful atmosphere. The sliding glass doors put it but a step from the outdoor terraces. Three bedrooms provide fine sleeping facilities. In addition to the full bath with its vanity, there is an adjacent stall shower directly accessible from the outside. This is a great feature during the summer swimming months. Note the combination washer-dryer nearby. The attached carport with its big storage unit is a practical feature.

Design 51471
1,465 Sq. Ft.; 11,344 Cu. Ft.

● A summer cottage which will surely play its part well. Although basically a two-bedroom house, its sleeping and living potential is much greater. The large screened porch offers a full measure of flexibility. It supplements the living room as an extra informal living area, while also permitting its use as a sleeping porch. Whatever its function, the screened porch certainly will be in constant use. Separating the living and dining rooms is the appealing raised hearth fireplace. A snack bar is handy to the kitchen which features a glass gable above the wall cabinets. This will be an efficient and cheerful place in which to work. A utility room houses the heating equipment and the combination washer-dryer. Sloping, beamed ceilings help maintain an aura of spaciousness throughout.

● After building this impressive design as your second home, you couldn't go wrong if you then proceeded to make this your first, and only, home. It is just big enough to take care of the growing, active family; while just small enough to serve admirably as a retirement home when the children are on their own – yet come back for visits on weekends or holiday vacations. There are three bedrooms, two full baths, a family room, living room and formal dining area. There is an attractive raised hearth fireplace, sloped ceilings throughout, carport with storage area and an abundance of glass.

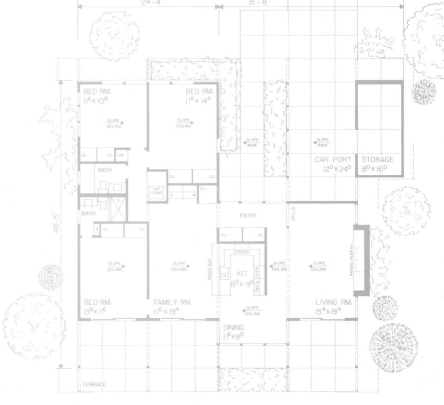

Design 53184
1,488 Sq. Ft.; 15,371 Cu. Ft.

● The features of this two bedroom leisure-time home are legion.
Its contemporary exterior, charac-
terized by the low-pitched, wide
overhanging roof, the masonry
masses, the dramatic glass areas
and the plan's irregular configuration, has a special appeal of its
own. The front privacy wall helps
form a delightful court. The development of this outdoor living area
can be a pleasant summer-time
project. Activities on and around
the rear covered porch and terraces will be enjoyable ones, indeed. Inside, there is an atmosphere of spaciousness enhanced
by the sloping ceilings.

Design 53185
1,222 Sq. Ft.; 11,707 Cu. Ft.

Design 51467
800 Sq. Ft.; 9,336 Cu. Ft.

● Here is a heap of vacation home living, all designed into a delightful cottage for a narrow site. The floor plan features two bedrooms, plus two bunk rooms. Then, there is a large living area with sliding glass doors, a glass gable end, sloped beamed ceiling and fireplace. There is a completely functional kitchen, a full bath and an outside bulk storage room.

● Your family will feel right at home, away from home, when they begin their stay at this smart cottage. The children will have two sizable bedrooms, while the parents will have their master bedroom with adjacent bath. Observe how this bath is also but a few steps from the side yard. The main bath is centrally located and conveniently contains the washer and dryer. Note living area.

Design 52410
1,130 Sq. Ft.; 10,998 Cu. Ft.

Design 52404
720 Sq. Ft.; 6,600 Cu. Ft.

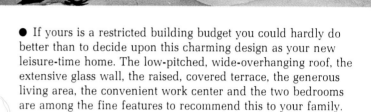

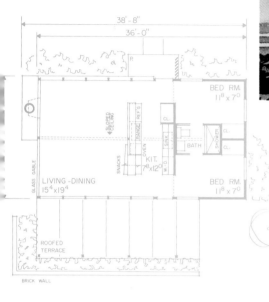

● If yours is a restricted building budget you could hardly do better than to decide upon this charming design as your new leisure-time home. The low-pitched, wide-overhanging roof, the extensive glass wall, the raised, covered terrace, the generous living area, the convenient work center and the two bedrooms are among the fine features to recommend this to your family.

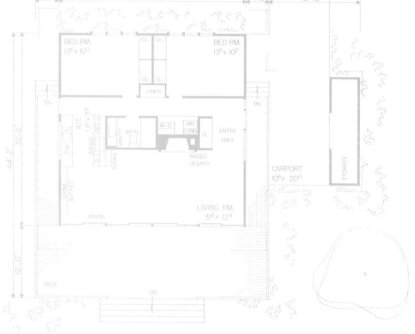

● This attractive second home will adapt wonderfully to its surroundings – whatever the setting. The big, wood deck will be just the place to enjoy the many hours of the day. Should you step back through the sliding glass doors, your view of the lake from the 31 foot living room would be only slightly impaired. The two bedrooms will make excellent bunk rooms to accommodate more vacationers.

Design 51419
1,040 Sq. Ft.; 10,567 Cu. Ft.

69

Design 52434 1,376 Sq. Ft.; 13,388 Cu. Ft.

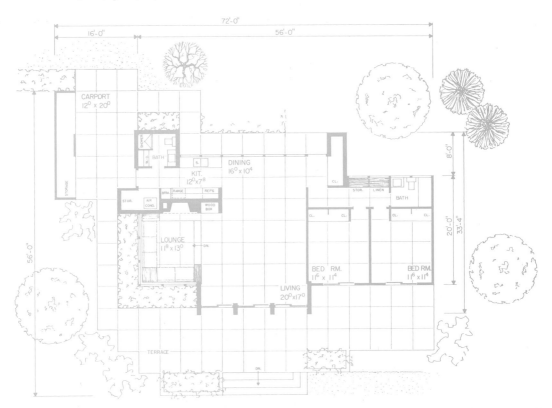

● It should be easy to visualize the fun and frolic you, your family, your guests and your neighbors will have in this home. The setting does not have to be near a bubbling brook, either. It can be almost any place where the pressures of urban life are far distant. The flat roof planes, the vertical brick piers, the massive chimney and the strategic glass areas are among the noteworthy elements of this design. Inside, there is space galore. The huge living-dining area flows down into the cozy, sunken lounge. The sleeping area of two bedrooms, a bath and good storage facilities is a zone by itself. The kitchen is efficient and has the bath and laundry equipment nearby. Imagine the spacious living area that runs from the front to the back of the house.

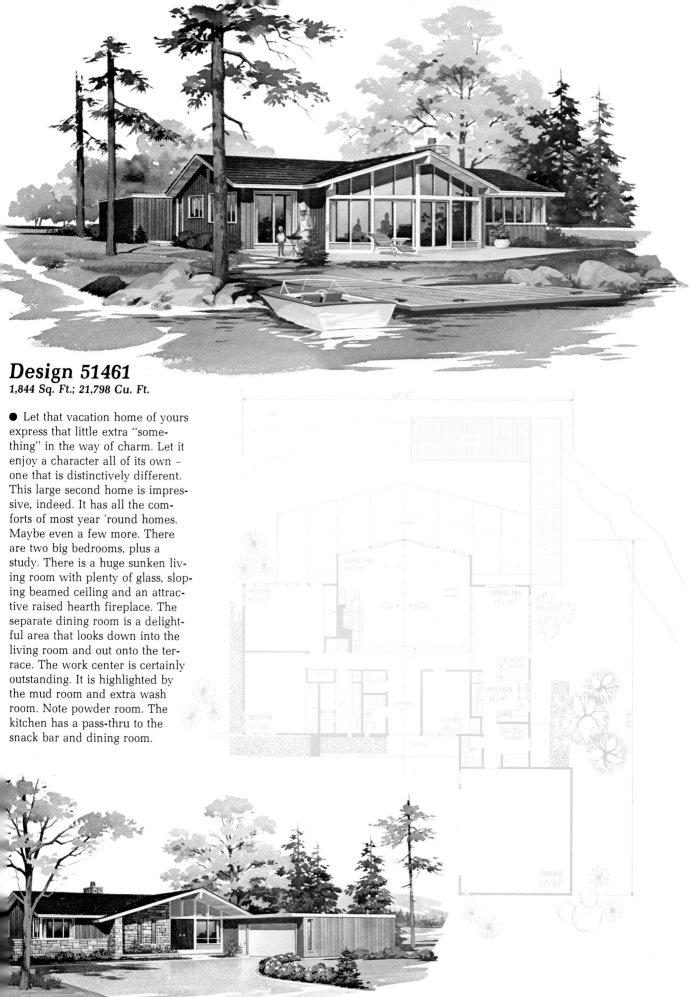

Design 51461
1,844 Sq. Ft.; 21,798 Cu. Ft.

● Let that vacation home of yours express that little extra "something" in the way of charm. Let it enjoy a character all of its own – one that is distinctively different. This large second home is impressive, indeed. It has all the comforts of most year 'round homes. Maybe even a few more. There are two big bedrooms, plus a study. There is a huge sunken living room with plenty of glass, sloping beamed ceiling and an attractive raised hearth fireplace. The separate dining room is a delightful area that looks down into the living room and out onto the terrace. The work center is certainly outstanding. It is highlighted by the mud room and extra wash room. Note powder room. The kitchen has a pass-thru to the snack bar and dining room.

Design 51492
608 Sq. Ft. – First Floor
120 Sq. Ft. – Second Floor; 12,084 Cu. Ft.

● It will not matter one bit where this log cabin is built, for there will be many paths beaten to its doors. The massive stone chimney seems to foretell of the warm hospitality awaiting inside. The big living area is dominated, as well it should be, by the centered fireplace.

● The rustic charm of this 40' x 20' rectangle will be hard to beat. Its appeal is all the more enticing when all that livability is the result of such economy of construction. In addition to the two bedrooms, there are two bunk rooms. Then, there is the big living/dining area with fireplace.

Design 51489
800 Sq. Ft.; 9,432 Cu. Ft.

Design 51487
708 Sq. Ft.; 10,337 Cu. Ft.

● The log cabin is hardly likely to pass from the American scene. Of course, its appropriate setting has long since ceased to be Main Street. This unmatched, rugged, appearance is in perfect harmony with the backwoods environment. Inside there is plenty of bunking and living space.

The charm of rustic vacation living is hardly better exemplified than by this half-log cabin with its massive stone chimney and its wide overhanging roof. Well-planned to accommodate a gang, the living area extends from front to rear. There's an abundance of space to enjoy the cozy fireplace.

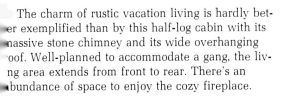

Design 51493
704 Sq. Ft.; 7,744 Cu. Ft.

Design 51430
1,296 Sq. Ft.; 13,284 Cu. Ft.

● This perfectly square vacation home has plenty of exterior appeal which surrounds an interesting, informal and smoothly functioning floor plan. The carport appendage and the fence add further interest to the exterior appeal and result in extra storage space and the development of a garden court. The informal atmosphere of the interior is enhanced by the walls of glass and the open planning.

● The keynote of vacation is fun. So what could be more appropriate than a vacation house that breaks away from ordinary design conventions? The most interesting nonconformity is the angled front and back walls. These angles are as important to the floor plan as they are to the design. They give the house its greatest width where it's most needed – across the living area. Note sloping ceilings.

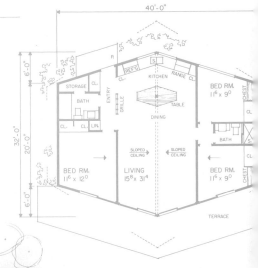

Design 51438
1,040 Sq. Ft.; 10,223 Cu. Ft.

Design 51418
805 Sq. Ft.; 7,647 Cu. Ft.

● An economically built rectangle that will be fun to construct as a family summer project. The bunk rooms with their built-in storage units will more than adequately serve the children. The main bedroom highlights long book shelves. The bath is compartmented to permit access to the stall shower from the outside – an excellent feature for bathers. The living area is an almost complete square.

● Despite its small size, six persons can live in this delightful vacation house; and it can accommodate even more if you install bunks instead of beds. Each bedroom has at least one closet, and the largest has two plus a built-in chest. All three bedrooms are grouped around a full bathroom. A 12'-long kitchen with wall cabinet space adjoins a large living area which has a fireplace.

Design 51414
768 Sq. Ft.; 7,933 Cu. Ft.

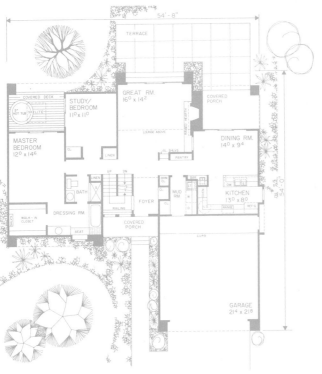

Design 52822
1,363 Sq. Ft. - First Floor
351 Sq. Ft. - Second Floor
36,704 Cu. Ft.

● Here is a truly unique house whose interior was designed with the current decade's economies, life-styles and demographics in mind. While functioning as a one-story home, the second floor provides an extra measure of livability when required. In addition, this two-story section adds to the dramatic appeal of both the exterior and the interior. Within only 1,363 square feet, this contemporary delivers refreshing and outstanding living patterns for those who are buying their first home, those who have raised their family and are looking for a smaller home and those in search of a retirement home.

ALTERNATE SECOND FLOOR

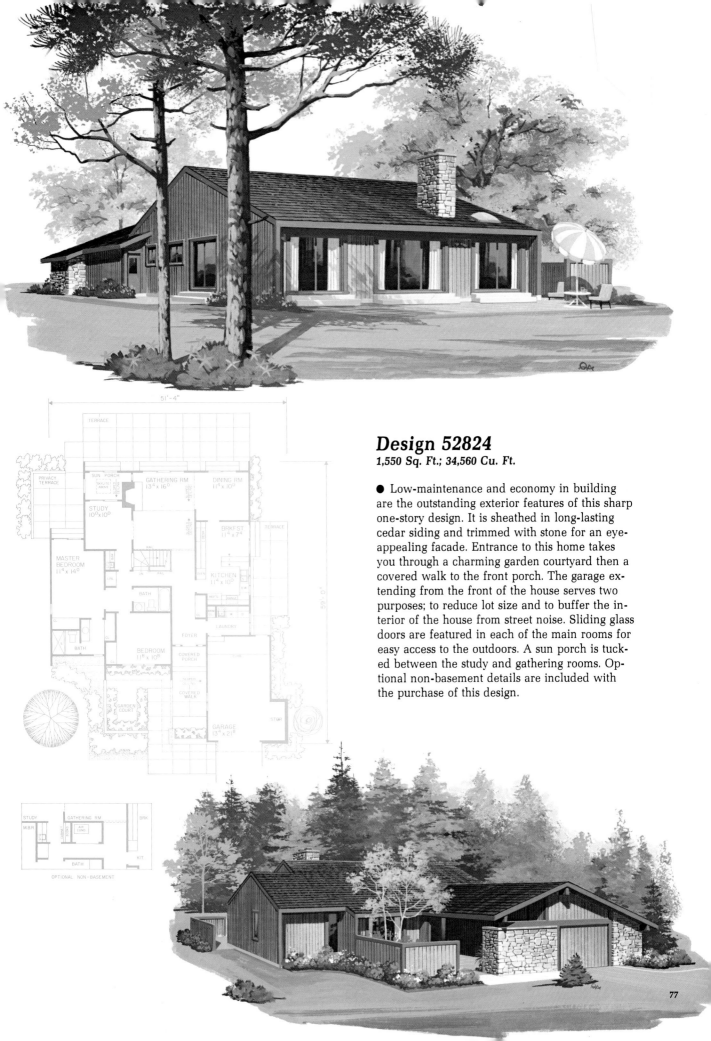

Design 52824
1,550 Sq. Ft.; 34,560 Cu. Ft.

● Low-maintenance and economy in building
are the outstanding exterior features of this sharp
one-story design. It is sheathed in long-lasting
cedar siding and trimmed with stone for an eye-
appealing facade. Entrance to this home takes
you through a charming garden courtyard then a
covered walk to the front porch. The garage ex-
tending from the front of the house serves two
purposes; to reduce lot size and to buffer the interior of the house from street noise. Sliding glass
doors are featured in each of the main rooms for
easy access to the outdoors. A sun porch is tucked between the study and gathering rooms. Optional non-basement details are included with
the purchase of this design.

Design 52565
1,540 Sq. Ft.; 33,300 Cu. Ft.

● This modest sized floor plan has much to offer in the way of livability. It may function as either a two or three bedroom home. The living room is huge and features a fine, raised hearth fireplace.

The open stairway to the basement is handy and will lead to what may be developed as the recreation area. In addition to the two full baths, there is an extra wash room. Adjacent is the laundry room and the service entrance from the garage.

The blueprints that you order for this design will show details for each of the three delightful elevations above. Which is your favorite? The Tudor, the Colonial or the Contemporary?

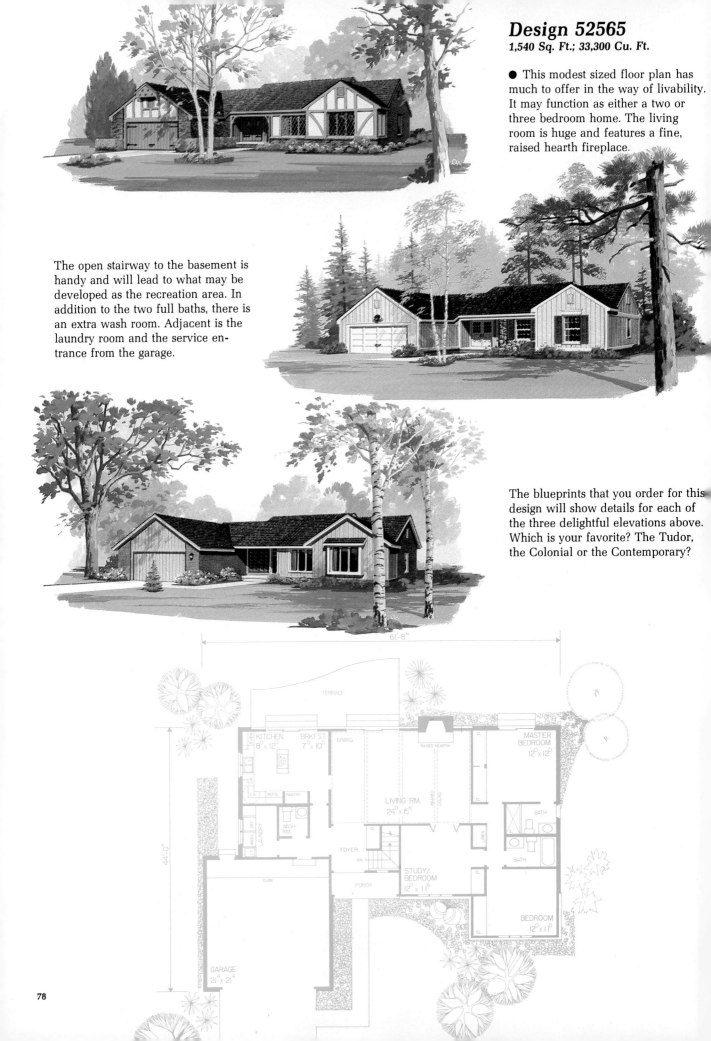

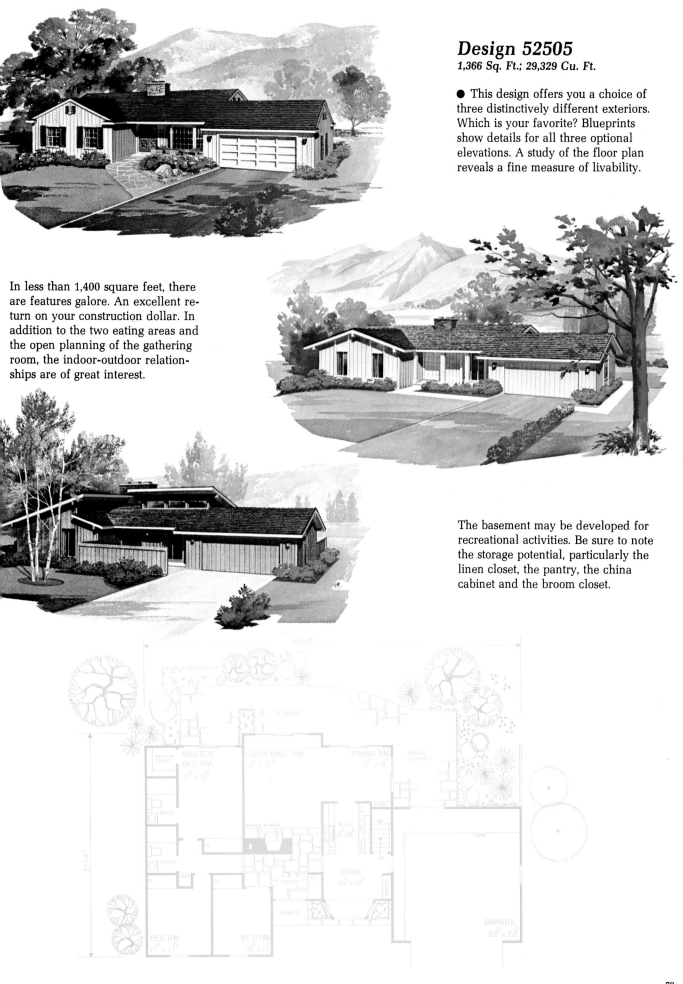

Design 52505
1,366 Sq. Ft.; 29,329 Cu. Ft.

● This design offers you a choice of three distinctively different exteriors. Which is your favorite? Blueprints show details for all three optional elevations. A study of the floor plan reveals a fine measure of livability.

In less than 1,400 square feet, there are features galore. An excellent return on your construction dollar. In addition to the two eating areas and the open planning of the gathering room, the indoor-outdoor relationships are of great interest.

The basement may be developed for recreational activities. Be sure to note the storage potential, particularly the linen closet, the pantry, the china cabinet and the broom closet.

Design 52432 984 Sq. Ft.; 10,627 Cu. Ft.

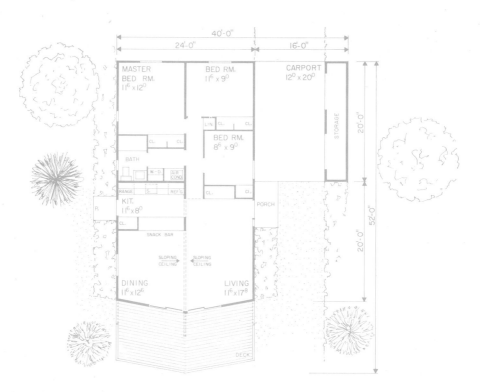

● Here is positive proof that even the most simple of floor plans can be long on livability and can be sheltered by a remarkably pleasing exterior. The 24 foot width of this second home is complemented by the 16 foot carport. The extension of the low-pitched roof to form the carport is a pleasing feature. The carport will double as a storage area for the boat while the storage wall will take care of all that fishing, boating, hunting and other recreational paraphernalia. The interior of this home is a model in the efficient use of space. None of it is wasted. There are plenty of closets; a fine, workable kitchen; a big counter snack bar; and sloping ceiling. You will cherish the hours spent on the wood deck. It is the ideal spot to sit back, relax and take in the beauty of the surrounding.

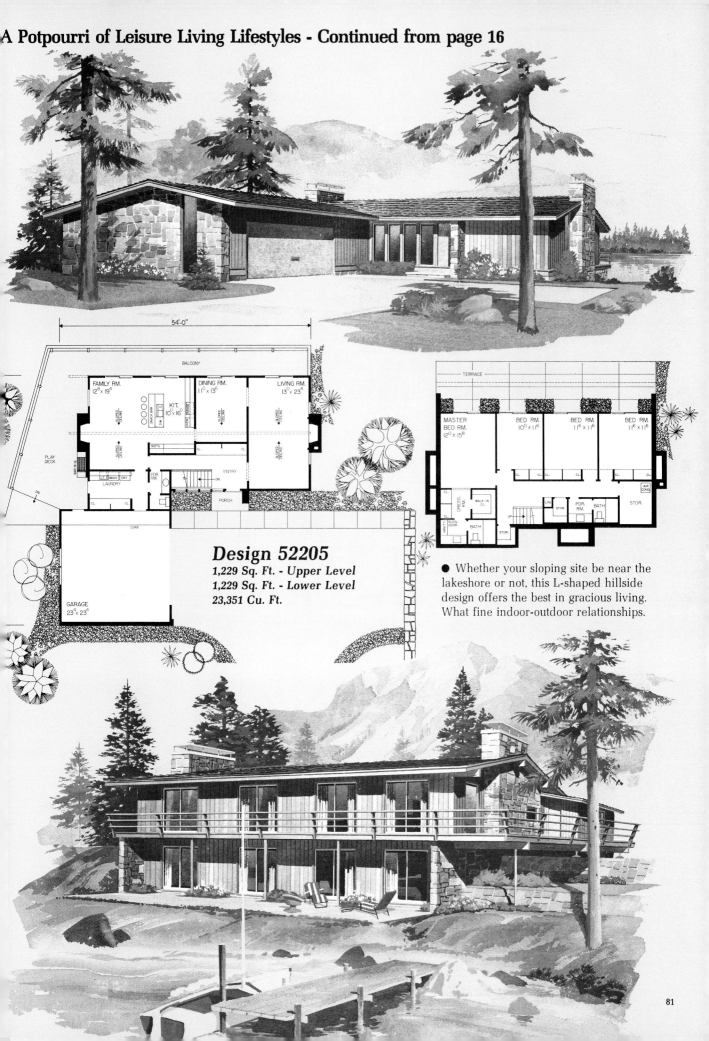

54'-0"

BALCONY

FAMILY RM.
12⁸ x 19⁴

DINING RM.
11⁰ x 13⁶

LIVING RM.
13⁰ x 23⁴

KIT.
10⁰ x 16⁰

SNACK BAR

PLAY DECK

SLOPED CEILING

SLOPED CEILING

SLOPED CEILING

SLOPED CEILING

REFG.

CL.

BAR-B-Q

WASH DRY

PDR. RM.

ENTRY

LAUNDRY

CL.

PORCH

CURB

GARAGE
23⁴ x 23⁴

TERRACE

MASTER BED RM.
12⁰ x 15⁸

BED RM.
10⁰ x 11⁶

BED RM.
11⁶ x 11⁶

BED RM.
11⁶ x 11⁶

CL. CL. CL. CL. CL. CL.

AIR COND.

DRESS. RM.

WALK-IN CL.

VANITY

SLDG. DOOR

BATH

STOR.

LIN.

STOR.

PDR. RM.

BATH

STOR.

STOR.

Design 52205
1,229 Sq. Ft. - Upper Level
1,229 Sq. Ft. - Lower Level
23,351 Cu. Ft.

● Whether your sloping site be near the lakeshore or not, this L-shaped hillside design offers the best in gracious living. What fine indoor-outdoor relationships.

Design 51499 *896 Sq. Ft. - Main Level; 298 Sq. Ft. - Upper Level; 896 Sq. Ft. - Lower Level; 18,784 Cu. Ft.*

● Three level living results in family living patterns which will foster a delightful feeling of informality. Upon arrival at this charming second home, each family member will enthusiastically welcome the change in environment – both indoors and out. Whether looking down into the living room from the dormitory balcony, or walking through the sliding doors onto the huge deck, or participating in some family activity in the game room, everyone will count the hours spent here as relaxing ones. Study the plan carefully.

Note the sleeping facilities on each of the three levels. Two bedrooms and a dormitory in all to sleep the family an friends comfortably. There are two fu baths, a separate laundry room and plenty of storage. Don't miss the efficient U-shaped kitchen.

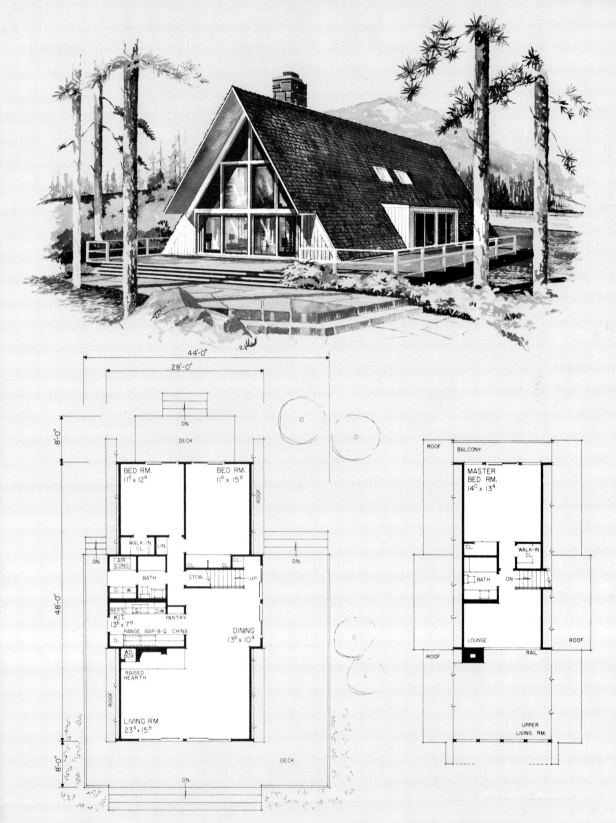

Design 51451 *1,224 Sq. Ft. - First Floor; 464 Sq. Ft. - Second Floor; 15,912 Cu. Ft.*

● This dramatic A-frame will surely command its share of attention wherever located. Its soaring roof and large glass areas put this design in a class all of its own. Raised wood decks on all sides provide delightful outdoor living areas. In addition, there is a balcony outside the second floor master bedroom. The living room will be the focal point of the interior. It will be wonderfully spacious with all that glass and the high roof. The attractive raised hearth fireplace will be a favorite feature. Another favored highlight will be the lounge area of the second floor where it is possible to look down into the living room. The work center has all the conveniences of home. Note the barbecue unit, pantry and china cabinet which are sure to help provide ease of living.

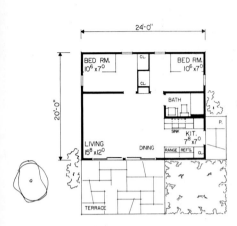

Design 51486
480 Sq. Ft.; 4,118 Cu. Ft.

● You'll be anxious to start building this delightful little vacation home. Whether you do-it-yourself, or engage professional help, you will not have to wait long for its completion.

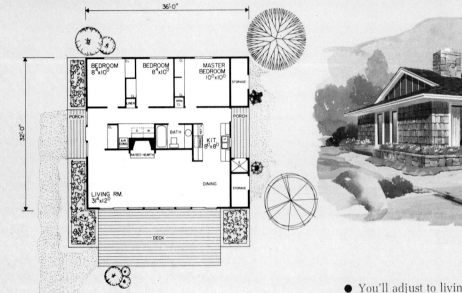

Design 52425
1,106 Sq. Ft.; 14,599 Cu. Ft.

● You'll adjust to living in this vacation cottage with the greatest of ease. And forevermore the by-word will be, "fun". Imagine, a thirty-one foot living room with access to a large deck!

Design 51449
1,024 Sq. Ft.; 11,264 Cu. Ft.

● If yours is a preference for a vacation home with a distinctive flair, then you need not look any further. Here is a simple and economically built 32 foot rectangle to meet your needs.

Design 51488
720 Sq. Ft.; 8,518 Cu. Ft.

● The kids won't be able to move into this vacation retreat soon enough. Two bunk rooms plus another bedroom for Mom and Dad. Open-planned living area. A real leisure-time home.

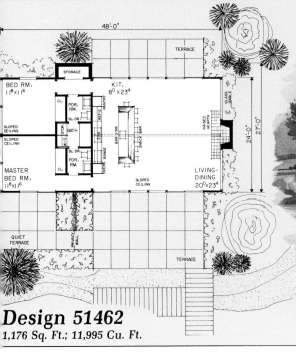

Design 51462
1,176 Sq. Ft.; 11,995 Cu. Ft.

● A second home with the informal living message readily apparent both inside and out. The zoning of this home is indeed most interesting – and practical, too. Study the plan carefully.

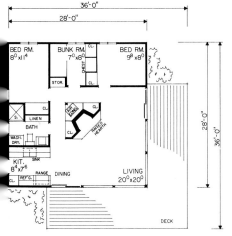

Design 51485
784 Sq. Ft.; 10,192 Cu. Ft.

● Here's a perfect 28 foot square that will surely open up new dimensions in living for its occupants. A fine, lower budget version of 51449 on the opposing page yet retaining many of the fine qualities.

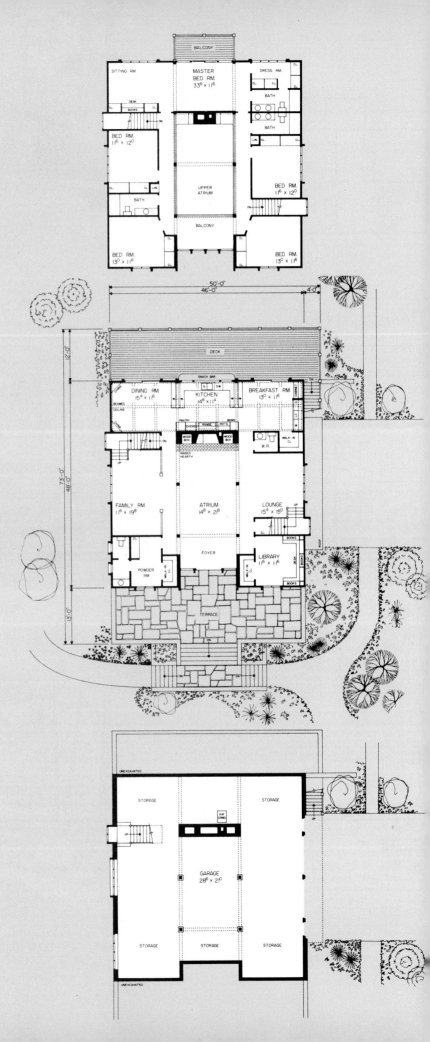

Design 52476

2,166 Sq. Ft. - First Floor
1,886 Sq. Ft. - Second Floor
78,289 Cu. Ft.

● Here is over 4,000 square feet of second home livability all wrapped-up in a two-story structure which is charmingly barnlike in character. The grand scale of this design is reminiscent of the increasingly popular project of remodeling the old, abandoned barn. Placed in its rural environment, the result is a peaceful setting for leisure home living. If your favorite old barn is not available for renovation, or hardly lends itself to such a project because of its location or its basic configuration, you need not despair. The blueprints for this design can be your first step to a new barnlike vacation home located wherever you may choose. As for the livability, the interior features unsurpassed informal living potential. The five bedroom second floor balcony looks down into the huge living area. The massive raised hearth fireplace may be enjoyed from the family room as well as the lounge area. The dining room-kitchen-breakfast room area highlights a beamed ceiling. Note outdoor snack bar. Other features include the library, the 33 foot master bedroom, the excellent bath facilities, the two flights of stairs to the second floor and the big basement area where the garage is located.

Barnlike In Character With Livability

On A Grand Scale

Design 52420

768 Sq. Ft. - Upper Level
768 Sq. Ft. - Lower Level
14,896 Cu. Ft.

● Two-level living can be fun anytime. When it comes to two-level living at the lake, seashore or in the woods, the experience will be positively delightful. Whether indoor or outdoor, family living will have a great opportunity for expression. Note two huge living areas, four bedrooms and two baths.

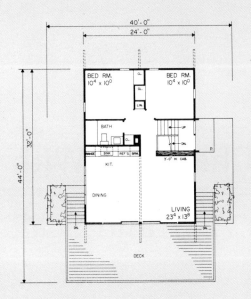

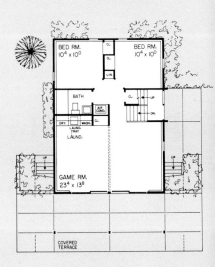

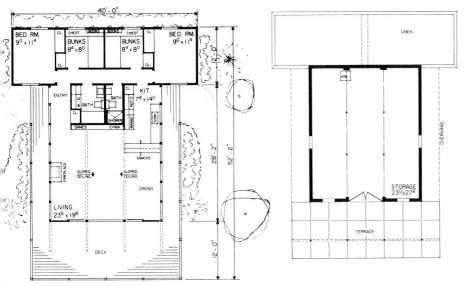

Design 51410
1,165 Sq. Ft.; 17,618 Cu. Ft.

● Wherever perched, this cottage will offer interesting and distinctive living patterns. The sleeping zone will enjoy its full measure of privacy. The bunk rooms and the two larger bedrooms provide plenty of sleeping space. Note the two baths. The cheerful, spacious living area is bounded on three sides by an outdoor balcony. The large glass areas, the sloping ceilings and the exposed beams make this a delightful area. Below the living area is a huge area for boat storage.

Design 51429
1,200 Sq. Ft. - Upper Level
646 Sq. Ft. - Lower Level
17,974 Cu. Ft.

● Build this weekend home right on the water. With two slips as part of its lower level, this design is a boating enthusiast's dream. Even those left behind after the boat has gone will love every moment spent relaxing on the upper deck with the water but a few feet below.

Design 51481

1,268 Sq. Ft. - First Floor
700 Sq. Ft. - Second Floor
18,112 Cu. Ft.

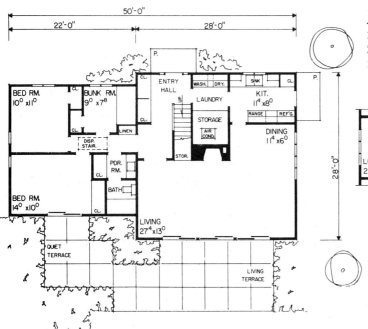

● Here are three second homes that retain much of the form, or shape, of traditional New England design to which present day window treatment has been added. The result is a pleasing mixture of the old and the new. Study the plans carefully. Livability is exceptional.

Design 51479

1,360 Sq. Ft.; 17,026 Cu. Ft.

● This unique plan is basically two 20 x 32 foot rectangles connected by an entrance hall, or passage unit. A sweeping wood deck provides the common outdoor living area. The sleeping unit has three bedrooms and two full baths. The ceiling of the master bedroom slopes.

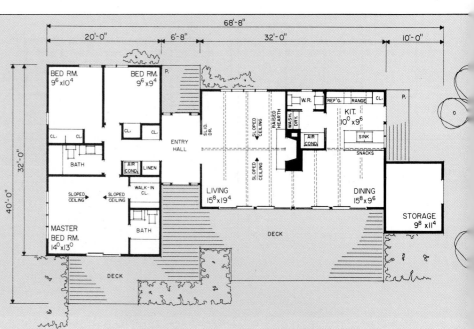

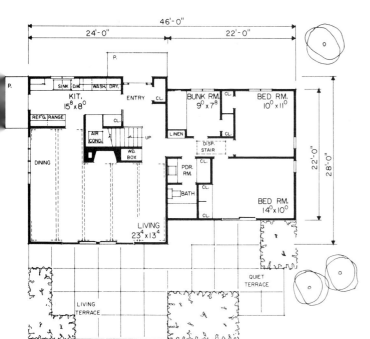

Design 51478

1,156 Sq. Ft. - First Floor
596 Sq. Ft. - Second Floor
15,656 Cu. Ft.

● Here is an abundance of vacation livability. Well zoned, there is a spacious beamed ceiling and dining area, an exceptional work center, a separate first floor sleeping wing. Upstairs there is the elegant master bedroom suite. For extra space don't miss the loft.

Design 51459

1,056 Sq. Ft. - First Floor
400 Sq. Ft. - Second Floor
17,504 Cu. Ft.

● There is a heap of vacation living awaiting the gang that descends upon this smart looking chalet adaptation. If you have a narrow site, this design will be of extra interest to you. Should one of your requirements be an abundance of sleeping facilities, you'd hardly do better in such an economically built design. There are three bedrooms downstairs. A ladder leads to the second floor loft. The children will love the idea of sleeping here. In addition, there is a play area which looks down into the first floor living room. A great vacation home.

Design 52427

784 Sq. Ft. - First Floor
504 Sq. Ft. - Second Floor
13,485 Cu. Ft.

● If ever a design had "vacation home" written all over it, this one has! Perhaps the most carefree characteristic of all is the second floor balcony which looks down into the wood deck. This balcony provides the outdoor living facility for the big master bedroom. Also occupying the second floor is the three-bunk dormitory. The use of bunks would be a fine utilization of this space. Panels through the knee walls give access to an abundant storage area. Downstairs there is yet another bedroom, a full bath and a 27 foot living room.

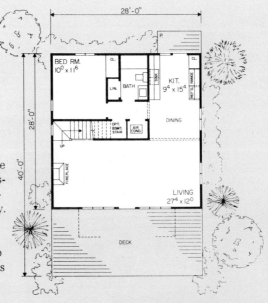

Design 51424

672 Sq. Ft. - First Floor
256 Sq. Ft. - Second Floor
8,736 Cu. Ft.

● This chalet-type vacation home with its steep, overhanging roof, will catch the eye of even the most casual onlooker. It is designed to be completely livable whether the season be for swimming or skiing. The dormitory of the upper level will sleep many vacationers, while the two bedrooms of the first floor provide the more convenient and conventional sleeping facilities. The upper level overlooks the living and dining area with its beamed ceiling. The lower level provides everything that one would want for vacation living.

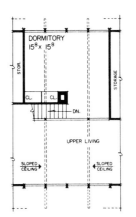

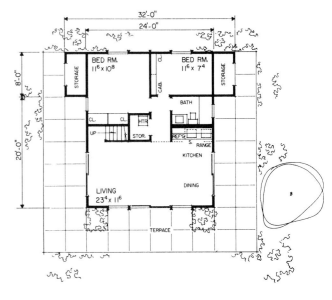

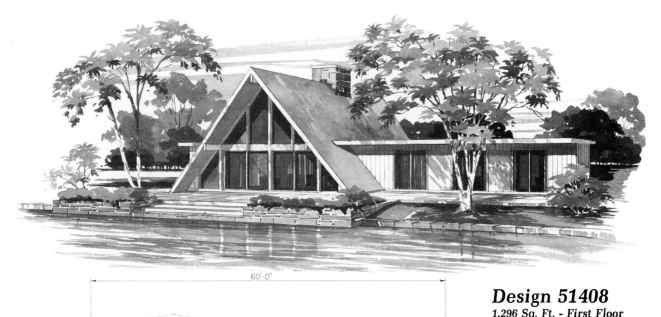

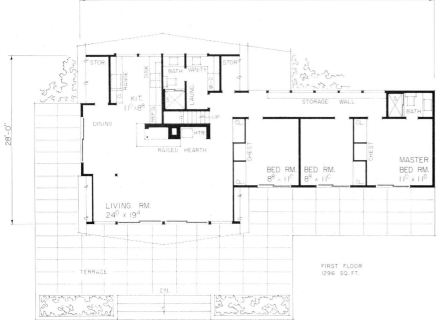

60'-0"

28'-0"

STOR.
RANGE
SINK
BATH VANITY
STOR.
W-D
KIT.
11⁰ x 8⁸
REFG.
LAUNC.
UP
STORAGE WALL
S
BATH
DINING
CL.
CHEST
CL.
CL.
CHEST
CL.
HTR.
RAISED HEARTH
BED RM.
8⁸ x 11⁰
BED RM.
8⁸ x 11⁰
MASTER
BED RM.
11⁰ x 11⁰
LIVING RM.
24⁰ x 19⁴

TERRACE

DN.

FIRST FLOOR
1296 SQ. FT.

Design 51408
1,296 Sq. Ft. - First Floor
181 Sq. Ft. - Second Floor
12,248 Cu. Ft.

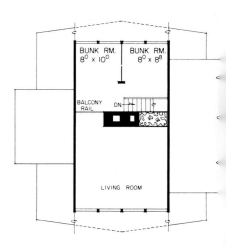

BUNK RM.
8⁰ x 10⁰
BUNK RM.
8⁰ x 8⁸
BALCONY
RAIL
DN.
LIVING ROOM

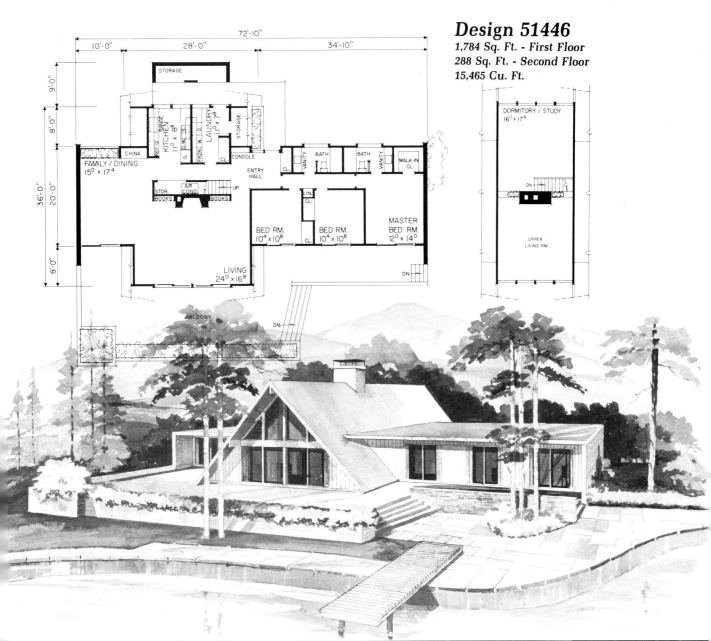

Design 51446

1,784 Sq. Ft. - First Floor
288 Sq. Ft. - Second Floor
15,465 Cu. Ft.

Design 51448

776 Sq. Ft. - First Floor
300 Sq. Ft. - Second Floor
8,596 Cu. Ft.

● Here are three dramatic A-frames designed to fit varying budgets and family living requirements. Compare the size of Design 51448 at left with that of 51446 above. While the difference in livability features is great, so is the difference in construction costs. However, the significance each design represents to the family's basic life style is similar. The proud owners of either home will enjoy all the benefits and experiences that come from leisure-time, second home living. Study the interior of 51408. It, too, has much to offer the fun oriented family during those special moments.

Build This Second Home
In Three Stages

Design 51425 576 Sq. Ft.; 5,553 Cu. Ft. - Basic Unit; 1,152 Sq. Ft.; 8,775 Cu. Ft. - Expanded Unit

● Here is a vacation home that can be easily built in three stages. This procedure will stretch your building budget and enable you to continue as your finances permit. Blueprints show details for the construction of the basic unit first. This features the kitchen, bath, bedroom and living room. The second stage can be either the addition of the two extra bedrooms, or the screened porch. Each addition is a modular 12 x 24 foot unit. The ceilings are sloping thus contributing to the feeling of spaciousness. The finished house has ex- cellent storage facilities. If desired, the screened porch could be modified to be built as a family room addition. Such a move would permit year 'round use. Note the perfectly rectangular shape of this home which will result in economical construction costs.

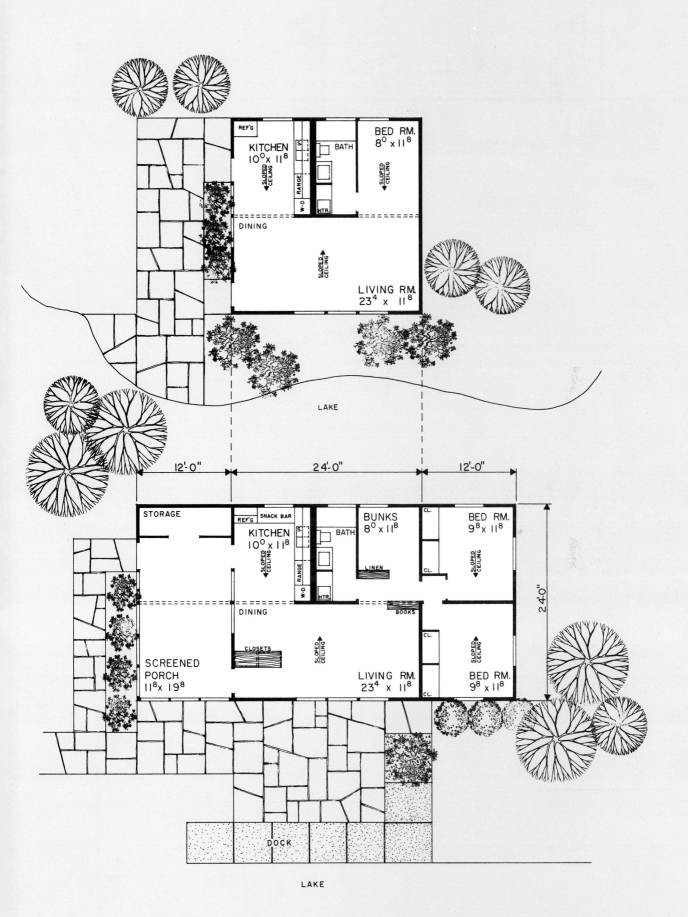

REF'G

KITCHEN
10⁰ x 11⁸

SLOPED CEILING

RANGE

W-D

HTR.

BATH

BED RM.
8⁰ x 11⁸

SLOPED CEILING

DINING

SLOPED CEILING

LIVING RM.
23⁴ x 11⁸

LAKE

12'-0" 24'-0" 12'-0"

STORAGE

REF'G SNACK BAR

KITCHEN
10⁰ x 11⁸

SLOPED CEILING

RANGE

W-D

HTR.

BATH

LINEN

BUNKS
8⁰ x 11⁸

CL.

CL.

BED RM.
9⁸ x 11⁸

SLOPED CEILING

DINING

BOOKS

CL.

24'-0"

SCREENED
PORCH
11⁸ x 19⁸

CLOSETS

SLOPED CEILING

LIVING RM.
23⁴ x 11⁸

CL.

SLOPED CEILING

BED RM.
9⁸ x 11⁸

DOCK

LAKE

97

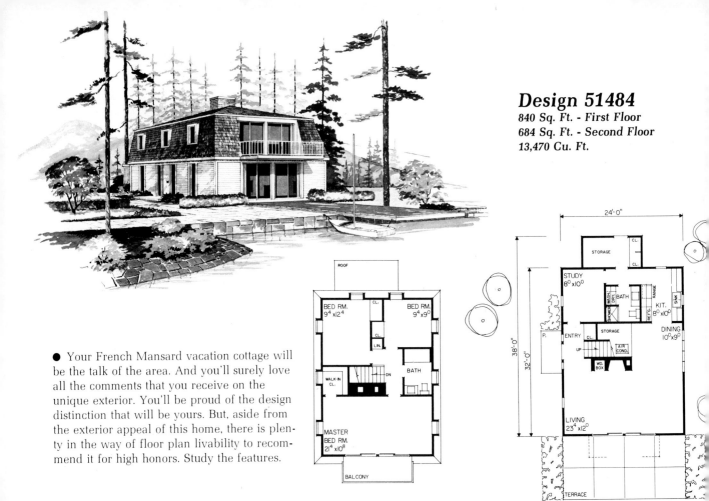

Design 51484

840 Sq. Ft. - First Floor
684 Sq. Ft. - Second Floor
13,470 Cu. Ft.

● Your French Mansard vacation cottage will be the talk of the area. And you'll surely love all the comments that you receive on the unique exterior. You'll be proud of the design distinction that will be yours. But, aside from the exterior appeal of this home, there is plenty in the way of floor plan livability to recommend it for high honors. Study the features.

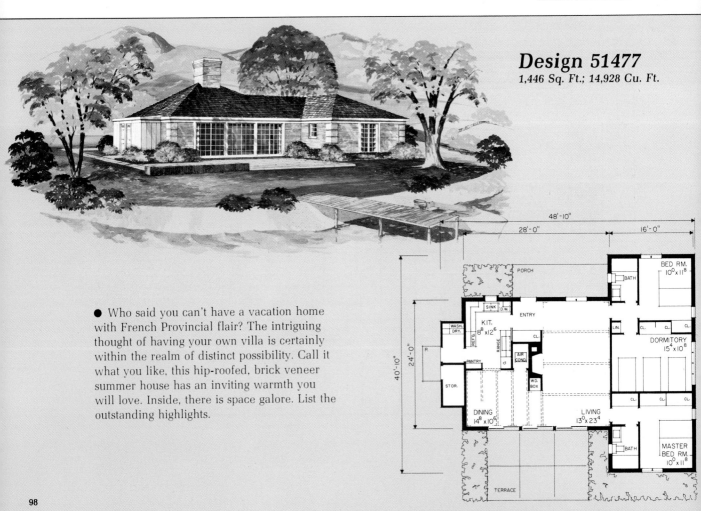

Design 51477

1,446 Sq. Ft.; 14,928 Cu. Ft.

● Who said you can't have a vacation home with French Provincial flair? The intriguing thought of having your own villa is certainly within the realm of distinct possibility. Call it what you like, this hip-roofed, brick veneer summer house has an inviting warmth you will love. Inside, there is space galore. List the outstanding highlights.

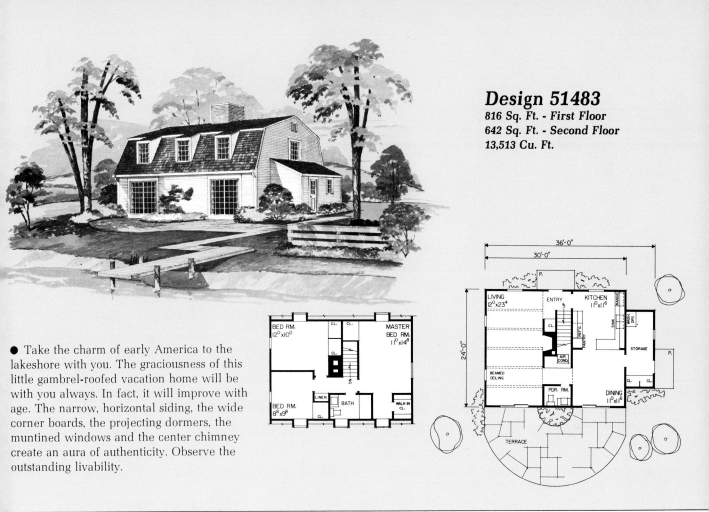

Design 51483
816 Sq. Ft. - First Floor
642 Sq. Ft. - Second Floor
13,513 Cu. Ft.

● Take the charm of early America to the lakeshore with you. The graciousness of this little gambrel-roofed vacation home will be with you always. In fact, it will improve with age. The narrow, horizontal siding, the wide corner boards, the projecting dormers, the muntined windows and the center chimney create an aura of authenticity. Observe the outstanding livability.

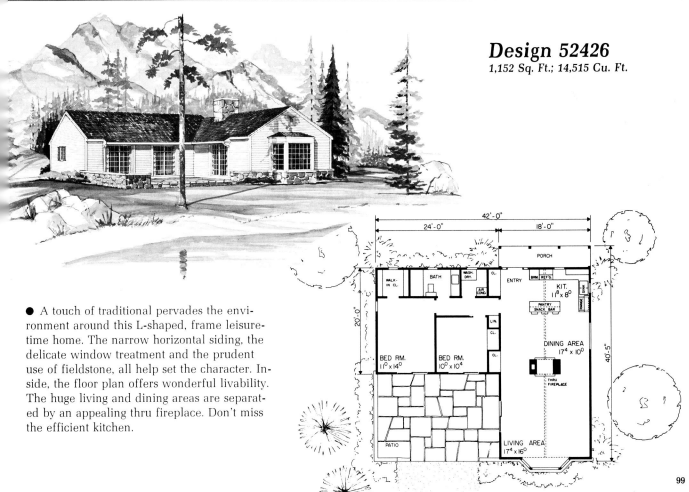

Design 52426
1,152 Sq. Ft.; 14,515 Cu. Ft.

● A touch of traditional pervades the environment around this L-shaped, frame leisure-time home. The narrow horizontal siding, the delicate window treatment and the prudent use of fieldstone, all help set the character. Inside, the floor plan offers wonderful livability. The huge living and dining areas are separated by an appealing thru fireplace. Don't miss the efficient kitchen.

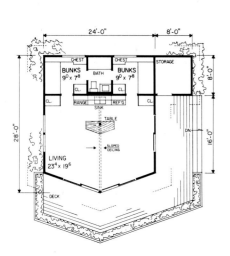

Design 51403 698 Sq. Ft.; 7,441 Cu. Ft.

Design 52424 1,456 Sq. Ft.; 16,760 Cu. Ft.

● Here are five outstanding second homes which, in spite of their variation in size, have many things in common. Perhaps the most significant common denominator is the location of the living area and its unrestricted view of the outdoors. Each of the designs feature a glass gable end and sloping ceiling which assures the living zone of a bright and cheerful atmosphere. A study of the sizes and the livability of these designs is interesting. They range in size from a 576 square foot, one bedroom cottage, to a 1,456 square foot lodge with four bedrooms plus two bunk rooms. Regardless of the overall size of the interior, the open planning of the living areas results in plenty of space for your family and visitors to just sit around and talk.

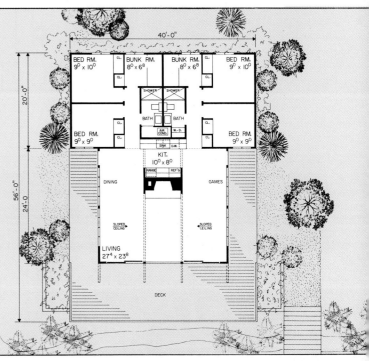

Design 52423 864 Sq. Ft.; 9,504 Cu. Ft.

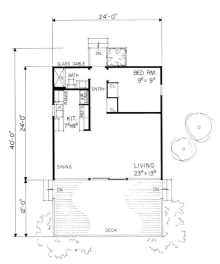

Design 51458 576 Sq. Ft.; 5,904 Cu. Ft.

Design 51495 800 Sq. Ft.; 9,108 Cu. Ft.

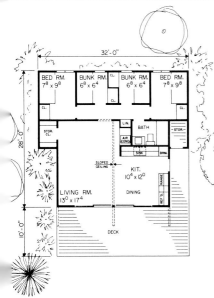

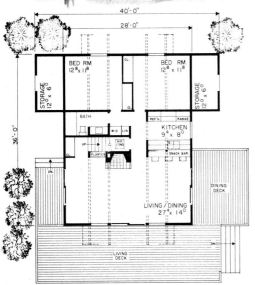

Design 51444

1,008 Sq. Ft. - First Floor
624 Sq. Ft. - Second Floor
15,542 Cu. Ft.

● Everybody will have fun spending their vacations at this cottage. And why shouldn't they? The pleasant experiences of vacation living will be more than just sitting on the outdoor balconies of the second floor. They will include eating leisurely on the dining deck and lounging peacefully on the living deck. Further, they will encompass the relaxing hours spent before the cheerful fireplace in the living room on cool evenings.

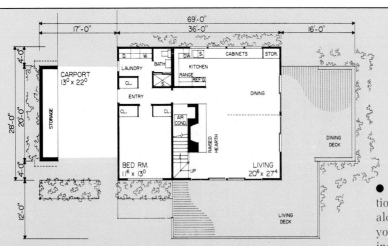

Design 51427

1,008 Sq. Ft. - First Floor
688 Sq. Ft. - Second Floor; 18,648 Cu. Ft.

● Imagine yourself living in this outstanding vacation home. Whether located deep in the woods or along the shore line, you will forever be aware of your glorious surroundings. As you relax in your living room you will enjoy the massive, raised hearth fireplace, the high-pitched beamed ceiling, the broad expanses of glass and the dramatic balcony looking down from above. List the features.

Design 51496

768 Sq. Ft. - First Floor
288 Sq. Ft. - Second Floor
15,840 Cu. Ft.

● If your vacation home desires include the wish for something distinctive in the way of exterior design,
you'll find this unique home a tempt-
ing choice. The overhanging shed
roof, the interesting glass areas and
the vertical siding help create an attractive facade. Inside, the living area
is big and spacious. Each floor features a good sized bedroom with a
full bath nearby. The ceiling is sloped and has exposed beams.

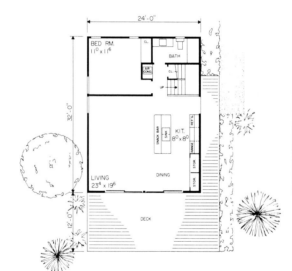

Design 51456
896 Sq. Ft.; 9,408 Cu. Ft.

● The big family should take notice of this outstanding cottage. Many hands will make the construction of this charming rectangle light work. And when the job is completed there will be plenty of space for everyone. In addition to the master bedroom, there are two other bedrooms. Each can take a bunk bed with plenty of space to spare. Note the excellent storage of the sleeping area. The living room will have a prefabricated fireplace with book shelves on each side. Note carport.

● This straightforward, three bedroom cottage features a fine lakefront exposure. Four sets of sliding glass doors open to the terraces. The side terrace is covered and because of its proximity to the kitchen will function conveniently as an eating terrace. Entry to the cottage from the street side is through one of the two large bulk storage areas. The living area is highlighted by the fireplace which is flanked by book shelves. The kitchen has plenty of counter space for the vacationing cook.

Design 51402
768 Sq. Ft.; 7,296 Cu. Ft.

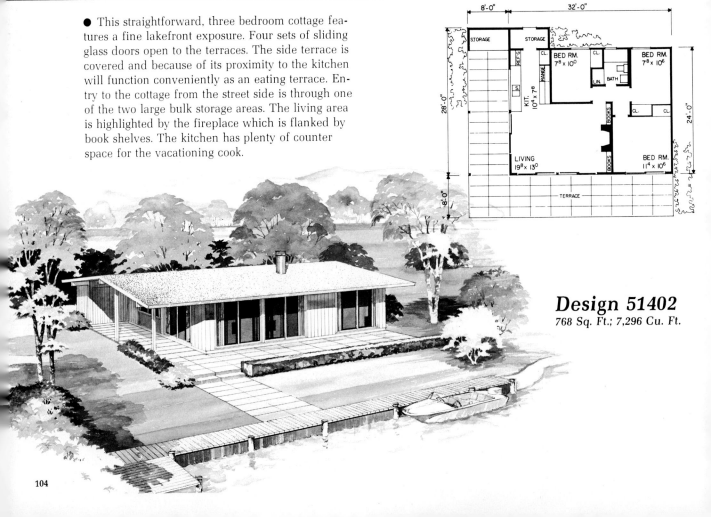

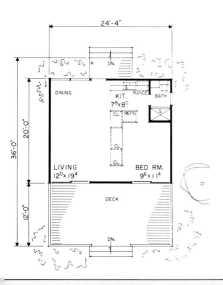

Design 51455 480 Sq. Ft.; 4,478 Cu. Ft.

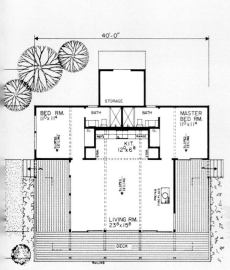

Design 51435 864 Sq. Ft.; 8,205 Cu. Ft.

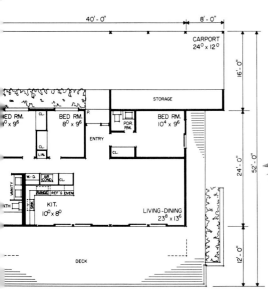

Design 51400 960 Sq. Ft.; 9,370 Cu. Ft.

Design 51426

1,396 Sq. Ft.; 14,441 Cu. Ft.

● You'll love the refreshingly new living patterns offered by this unique vacation home. A bright and cheerful center living core projects its glass areas toward the lake. Additional natural light is provided to this area through the skylight in the ceiling. An attractive built-in, a fireplace and twin closets also highlight this area. The sleeping facilities are postively outstanding. Each of the three bedrooms is of good size and functions through sliding glass doors with the terrace area. A full bath is but a couple of steps from each bedroom. The fine kitchen is strategically located.

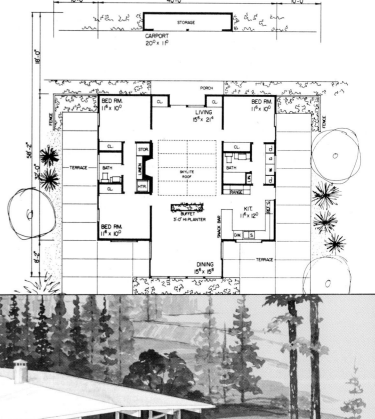

Design 51409

1,120 Sq. Ft.; 9,890 Cu. Ft.

● This flat-roofed, T-shaped leisure-time home proves the point that good zoning is good sense in any plan. It is interesting to note the practical result of two complete squares functioning together to provide convenient vacation living. The three bedroom, two full bath sleeping wing will enjoy its privacy from the spacious, open-planned, living area. The storage potential both inside and out is outstanding. Observe the built-in units. The raised hearth fireplace will be a favorite feature. The L-shaped deck will be a popular spot for young and old alike.

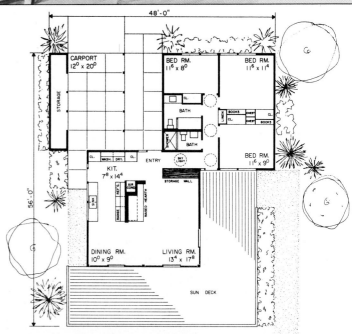

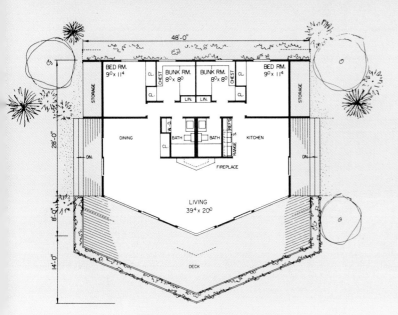

BED RM.
9⁰ x 11⁴

BUNK RM.
8⁰ x 8⁰

BUNK RM.
8⁰ x 8⁰

BED RM.
9⁰ x 11⁴

STORAGE

STORAGE

CL.
CHEST

CL.

LIN.
LIN.

CHEST
CL.

48'-0"

28'-0"

8'-0"

14'-0"

DINING

BATH
BATH

CL.
W.D.
RANGE
REF.
S.

KITCHEN

FIREPLACE

DN.
DN.

LIVING
39⁴ x 20⁰

DECK

Design 51413
1,200 Sq. Ft.; 13,005 Cu. Ft.

● The lake side of this interesting vacation home is reminiscent of the bow of a ship. The wall of glass angles forward to a point. This is, indeed, a dramatic feature of the spacious 39 foot living area. Four sets of sliding glass doors open onto the big deck which also is accessible from the kitchen and dining areas. Thoughtful planning results in the plumbing facilities being grouped together in the center of the house. Two full back-to-back baths service the two larger bedrooms and the two bunk rooms. Don't miss the storage.

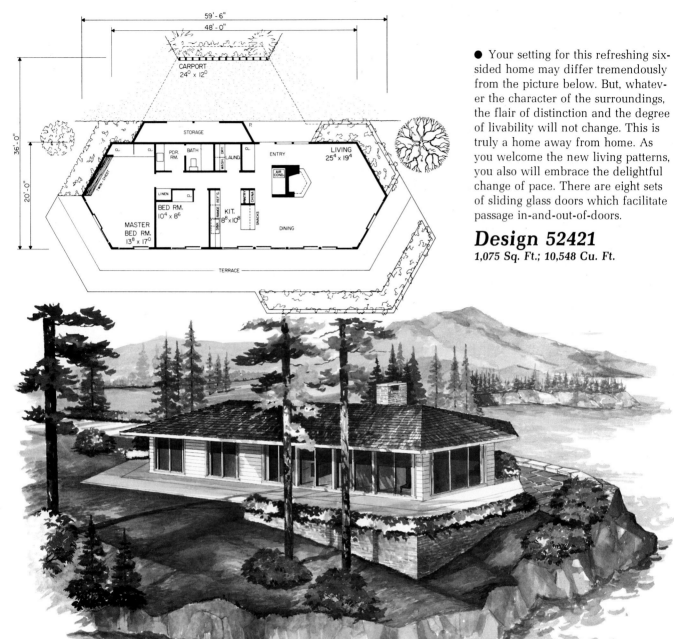

● Your setting for this refreshing six-sided home may differ tremendously from the picture below. But, whatever the character of the surroundings, the flair of distinction and the degree of livability will not change. This is truly a home away from home. As you welcome the new living patterns, you also will embrace the delightful change of pace. There are eight sets of sliding glass doors which facilitate passage in-and-out-of-doors.

Design 52421
1,075 Sq. Ft.; 10,548 Cu. Ft.

Design 51439
1,284 Sq. Ft.; 11,338 Cu. Ft.

● This handsome contemporary house is a far cry from the rough cabins we sometimes envision as vacation houses. It's truly designed for big family living with four bedrooms, two baths and a standard-sized kitchen. It also has the essential ingredients for cutting down maintenance, such as weathered board-and-batten siding and a windproof flat roof. There are many floor-to-ceiling windows to bring in the summer sunlight, and overhangs to keep out the sun's heat.

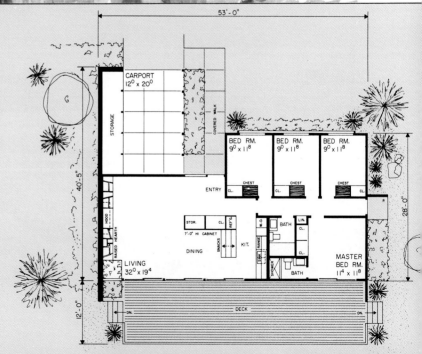

Design 51497

1,292 Sq. Ft.; 13,730 Cu. Ft.

● Another design whose general shape is most interesting and whose livability is truly refreshing. After a stay in this fine second home it will, indeed, be difficult to resume your daily activities in your first home. When you return from vacation you will miss the spaciousness of your living room, the efficiency of your work center, the pleasing layout of your master bedroom and all those glass sliding doors which mean you are usually but a step from the trouble-free out-of-doors.

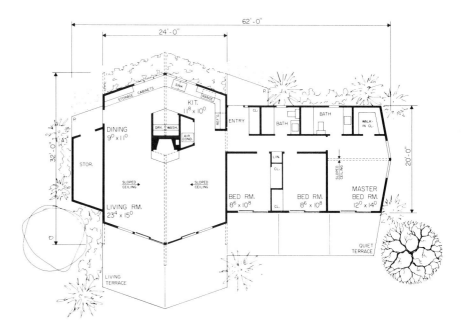

Design 51415

504 Sq. Ft. - First Floor
160 Sq. Ft. - Second Floor
9,576 Cu. Ft.

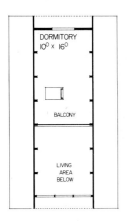

DORMITORY
10⁰ x 16⁰

BALCONY

LIVING
AREA
BELOW

18'-0"

BATH

BED RM.
8⁸ x 9⁸

STORAGE

RANGE
S. REF'G
KIT.
8⁰ x 6⁰

LADDER

CL.

CL.

DINING

28'-0"

44'-6"

LIVING
18⁰ x 15⁴

12'-0"

DECK

DN.

● These charming, low-cost A-frames will be hard to beat for carefree, informal living. The lakeside exteriors of these vacation homes feature delightfully vertical expanses of glass, thus affording unrestricted views of the outdoors. The large wood decks function with the living areas. Access to the second floor of each plan is by way of the ladder.

Design 51416

360 Sq. Ft. - First Floor
80 Sq. Ft. - Second Floor
5,888 Cu. Ft.

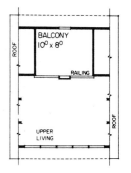

ROOF

BALCONY
10⁰ x 8⁰

RAILING

UPPER
LIVING

ROOF

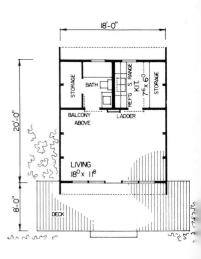

18'-0"

STORAGE

BATH

REF'G
S. RANGE
KIT.
7⁶ x 6⁰

STORAGE

BALCONY
ABOVE

LADDER

20'-0"

LIVING
18⁰ x 11⁸

8'-0"

DECK

CLUSTER UNITS . . .

are a unique and exciting approach to vacation home planning. They offer the opportunity to plan your home for development in stages with each unit extremely functional. As illustrated on the following pages, a starter unit may consist of a 484 square foot living-dining-kitchen-bedroom structure measuring 22x22 feet. As the family grows and financial constraints lessen, additional units may be added to accommodate additional bedrooms, a large lounge area, and even a garage. Passage units are utilized to attach all structures together. Blueprints are available for all units.

Design 52451
1,488 Sq. Ft.; 15,808 Cu. Ft.

● Here is a new dimension in vacation living. Three individual units connected by passageways result in a delightful cluster grouping with complete livability. From a design standpoint, clusters are most attractive and refreshing. On a basis of planning, they offer a wide range of living potential and flexibility. As for the budget, their expansible characteristics permit you to start your building program now with a small single structure and progress over the years, as funds become available, to a three, four or even five unit cluster compound. Study the plan at the right. Imagine your second home having a private, separate sleeping unit and an exciting spacious living area with a ceiling that slopes upward to a center skylight.

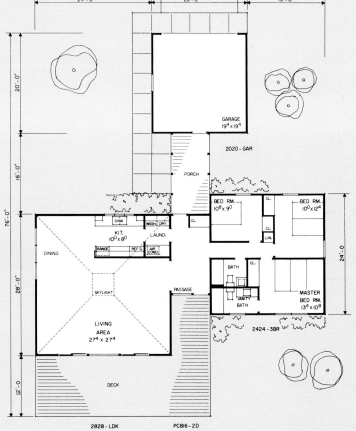

111

A NEW, EXCITING CONCEPT FOR DESIGNING AND BUILDING YOUR LEISURE LIVING PROJECT—
CLUSTER UNITS

● Now you can have fun being your own architectural designer. This unique vacation home series has been created with individual unit plans and exteriors for designing any number of cluster groupings to satisfy your own taste, budget and living requirements. If, at the beginning of your project, economy is your goal, you can build a single completely livable starter unit and add the other units later (see next two pages). However, if you want a luxurious vacation retreat now, you can combine a number of individual units (see inventory pages), each with specific luxury living space and features. Outdoor decks, terraces, landscaping and natural site beauty, can all be part of the overall final design by being your own creater of your vacation home.

BASIC TWO-UNIT DESIGN

● This small cluster is comprised of a single LDK (living-dining-kitchen) unit and a single 4 BR (four bedroom) unit, connected by a PC (passage-closet) unit. The LDK and 4 BR units are available in three sizes: 20 feet square (2020); 24 feet square (2424); 28 feet square (2828). If you wish, other units may be planned to be added from the cluster inventory. Wood decks or terraces are optional additions.

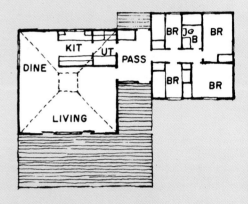

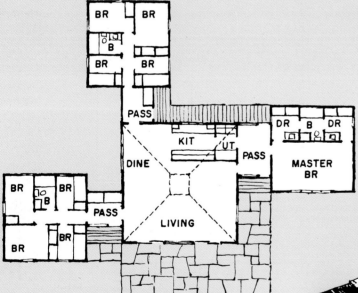

STAGGERED FOUR-UNIT DESIGN

● The versatility of the individual cluster unit planning idea is clearly illustrated in this spreading design. Maximum sleeping facilities, accommodating from 10 to 18 people, have been placed around the central living core. Note the luxury master bedroom suite with its private bath and twin dressing rooms.

● This cluster design looks like fun for all family members. And, indeed, living in it will be just that! To experience the immense indoor-outdoor enjoyment this cluster will offer, all you'll have to do is build it and move in.

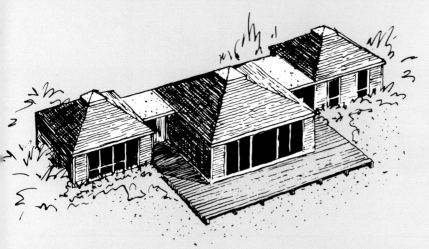

IN-LINE THREE UNIT DESIGN

● Locate your individual units side by side to result in an in-line cluster. Here, an LDK unit is flanked by a MBR unit and 3 BR unit. Two passage units and a deck provide for a flexible flow of traffic through the plan.

● The spreading wings of this cluster allow for the maximum enjoyment of sunshine and exposure. This symmetrical design affords gracious, healthful living throughout.

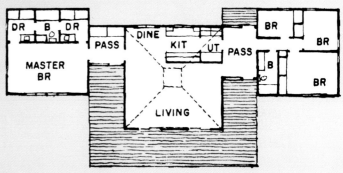

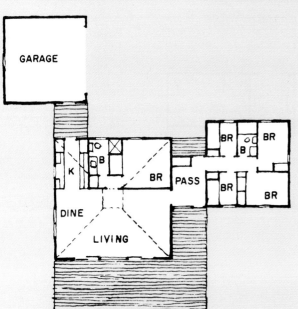

STAGGERED THREE UNIT DESIGN

● Shapes and living patterns can be made to be most interesting. This cluster is the result of adding to an LKBR-"Starter" unit, a 4 BR unit at the side and a GAR unit at the rear. Observe how this selection of units results in five bedrooms, two baths, living/dining/kitchen area and garage bulk storage.

IN-LINE THREE UNIT DESIGN

● The starter unit, LKBR, was the first structure planned for this cluster. Then, the spacious lounge with a massive, two-way fireplace, LOFP, was added. This 28 foot square area with its sloping ceilings on four sides will be ideal for entertaining the holiday gang. Finally, the three bedroom, two bath, 3 BR unit, was attached, thus allowing for even a greater extension of hospitality.

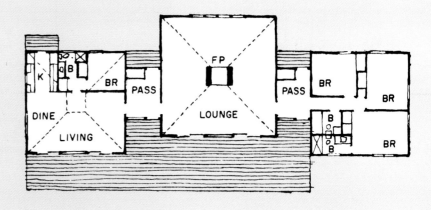

STARTER CLUSTER UNITS — COMPLETE LIVABILITY

Design 52445
964 Sq. Ft.; 9,844 Cu. Ft.

● All starter units are designed for the minimum budget, or for those who wish to build their cluster in stages. They are comprised of a living-dining area with sloping ceilings to the center skylight, an efficient kitchen, a bedroom and a full bath. In addition, space has been provided for the laundry, hot water and air-conditioning equipment. It is a complete living unit in itself. The addition of another unit can only add to its efficiency.

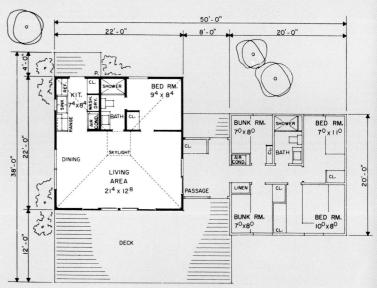

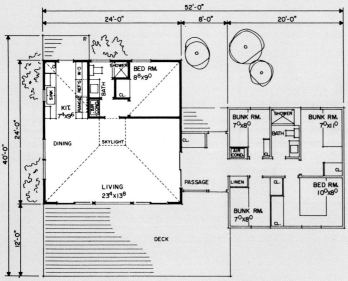

Design 52446
1,056 Sq. Ft.; 10,910 Cu. Ft.

● Starter units are available in four different sizes. Design 52445 has a starter unit measuring 22' x 22'; Design 52446 measures 24' x 24'; Design 52447 has starter unit dimensions of 26' x 26'; Design 52448 is 28' square. The attached four bedroom units and passage units are identical for each of the four designs. The blueprints you order for each design show details for the construction of the complete two-unit cluster. Build them one at a time if you wish.

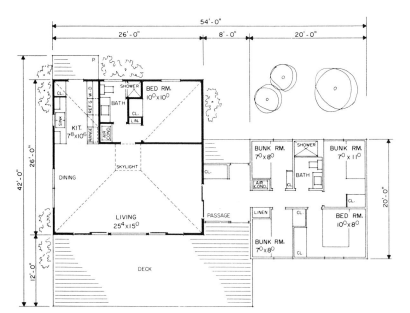

Design 52447
1,156 Sq. Ft.; 12,074 Cu. Ft.

● The construction of the sleeping unit 2020-4 BR, adds 400 square feet of living space to that of the starter unit. There are four bedrooms, a bath with stall shower and fine closet facilities. The use of double bunks means "welcome" to a few more overnight guests. Details for building the delightful outdoor wood deck are included in the blueprints.

Design 52448
1,264 Sq. Ft.; 13,380 Cu. Ft.

● Design 52448, at the right, is the largest of the four starter units on these pages. Its appeal, of course, is that its basic living unit is 28 feet square. Compare the size and livability of this design with the smaller 22 foot version, Design 52445. Observe the additional space of the living area and the bedroom. These units are ideal for ski or hunting lodges; in fact, all vacation living.

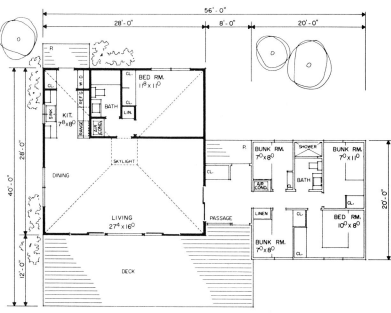

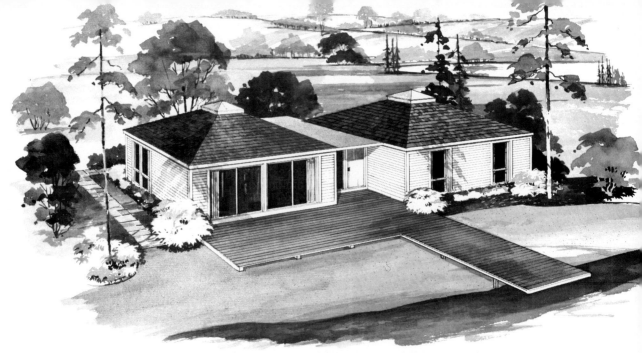

BASIC TWO-UNIT CLUSTERS—THREE SIZES

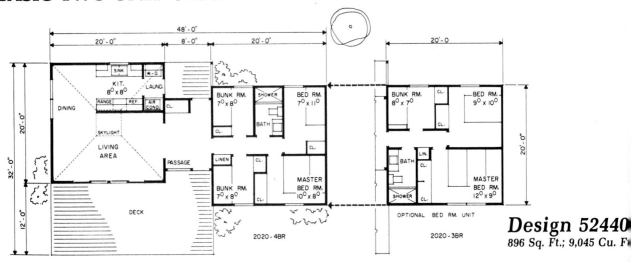

Design 52440
896 Sq. Ft.; 9,045 Cu. Ft.

● Home Planners' basic two-unit cluster designs are illustrated on these two pages in three different sizes. The LDK (living-dining-kitchen) units of these three designs are 20' x 20' for Design 52440; 24' x 24' for Design 52442; 28' x 28' for Design 52444. Connected to each LDK unit is an identically sized bedroom unit. The blueprints for Design 52440 and 52442 include complete details for building either the three four bedroom units. For the large sign 52444, details are included fo four or five bedroom units. Study design with your family.

The cross-section diagram below illustrates how the dramatic four-sided, sloping ceiling of all LDK (living-dining-kitchen) units are capped by a cheerful, ventilated skylight at the center. All bedroom units have flat ceilings with roof truss construction and ventilated cupolas at the top-center. They are similar in exterior design to the skylights of the LDK units.

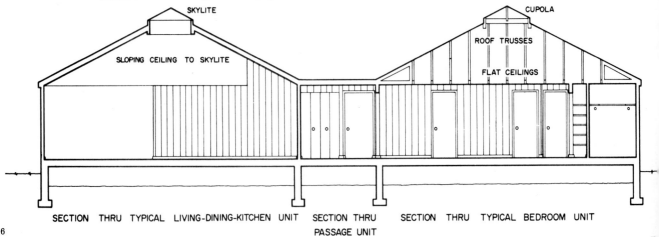

SECTION THRU TYPICAL LIVING-DINING-KITCHEN UNIT   SECTION THRU TYPICAL BEDROOM UNIT
PASSAGE UNIT

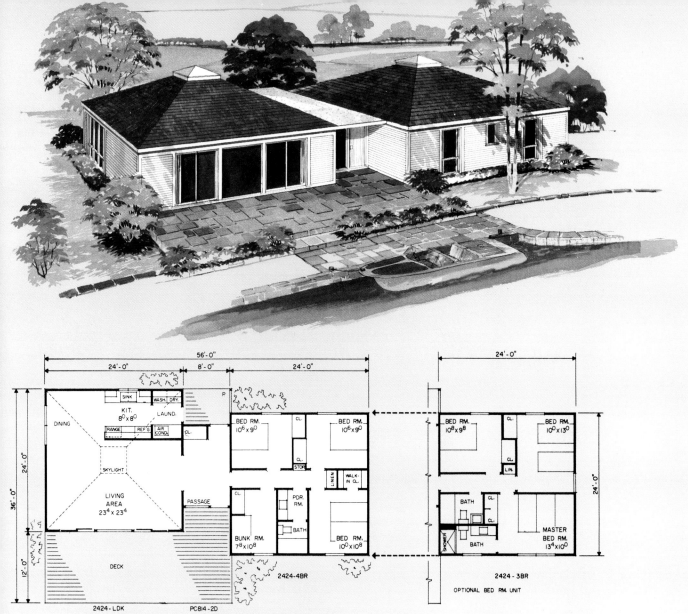

Design 52442 1,264 Sq. Ft.; 13,198 Cu. Ft.

Floor plan labels (Design 52442):

- 56'-0" overall; 24'-0", 8'-0", 24'-0"
- 36'-0", 24'-0", 12'-0"
- DINING
- KIT. 8⁰ x 8⁰
- SINK, WASH. DRY., LAUND.
- RANGE, REF'G, AIR COND.
- SKYLIGHT
- LIVING AREA 23⁴ x 23⁴
- PASSAGE
- DECK
- CL.
- BED RM. 10⁶ x 9⁰
- BED RM. 10⁶ x 9⁰
- CL.
- STOR.
- LINEN, WALK-IN CL.
- BUNK RM. 7⁸ x 10⁸
- PDR. RM.
- BATH
- BED RM. 10⁰ x 10⁸
- 2424-4BR
- 2424-LDK
- PC814-2D
- P

Optional Bed Rm. Unit (2424-3BR), 24'-0", 24'-0":
- BED RM. 10⁸ x 9⁸
- BED RM. 10⁰ x 13⁰
- CL., LIN.
- BATH, CL.
- SHOWER, BATH
- MASTER BED RM. 13⁴ x 10⁰
- OPTIONAL BED RM. UNIT

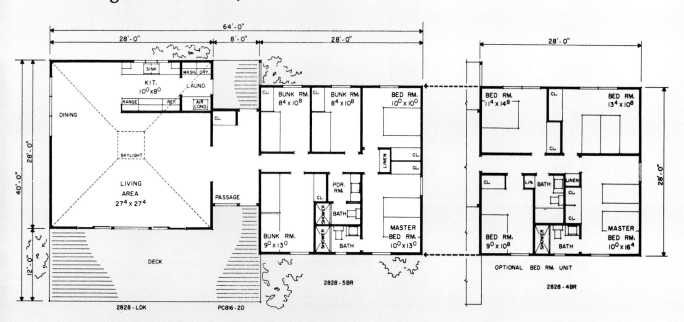

Design 52444 1,696 Sq. Ft.; 18,278 Cu. Ft.

Floor plan labels (Design 52444):

- 64'-0" overall; 28'-0", 8'-0", 28'-0"
- 40'-0", 28'-0", 12'-0"
- DINING
- KIT. 10⁰ x 8⁰
- SINK, WASH. DRY., LAUND.
- RANGE, REF., AIR COND.
- SKYLIGHT
- LIVING AREA 27⁴ x 27⁴
- PASSAGE
- DECK
- CL.
- BUNK RM. 8⁴ x 10⁸
- BUNK RM. 8⁴ x 10⁸
- BED RM. 10⁰ x 10⁰
- LINEN, CL.
- BUNK RM. 9⁰ x 13⁰
- PDR. RM., CL.
- SHOWER, SHOWER, BATH, BATH
- MASTER BED RM. 10⁰ x 13⁰
- 2828-5BR
- 2828-LDK
- PC816-2D

Optional Bed Rm. Unit (2828-4BR), 28'-0", 28'-0":
- BED RM. 11⁴ x 14⁸
- BED RM. 13⁴ x 10⁸
- CL., CL.
- CL., LIN., BATH, LINEN
- SHOWER, BATH, CL.
- BED RM. 9⁰ x 10⁸
- MASTER BED RM. 10⁰ x 16⁴
- OPTIONAL BED RM. UNIT

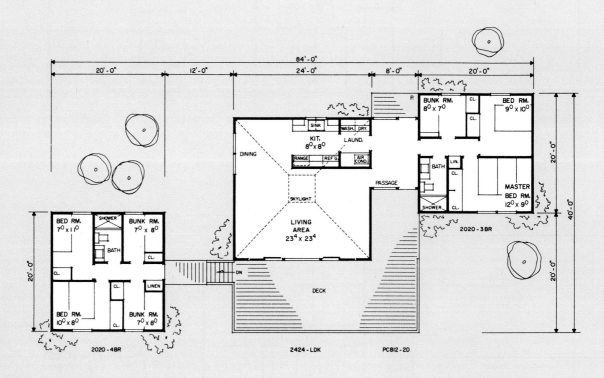

Design 52452 1,472 Sq. Ft.; 15,145 Cu. Ft.

● If you have been wondering how the cluster units may be oriented to function on a sloping site, here is one example of how this may be achieved. This cluster reveals two units attached by a standard passage unit, while a third unit, on a lower level, is accessi- ble down the deck stairs. Locating the living unit with its wood deck on high ground allows for the fullest enjoyment of the surrounding countryside. The adjacent three bedroom unit contains the master bedroom. The location of the detached unit may vary depending upon your site condition. This would matter little, for this unit may function as a bunk house. You may wish to consider locating your individual units on your site without attaching them with passage units. This design takes the best advantage of its site.

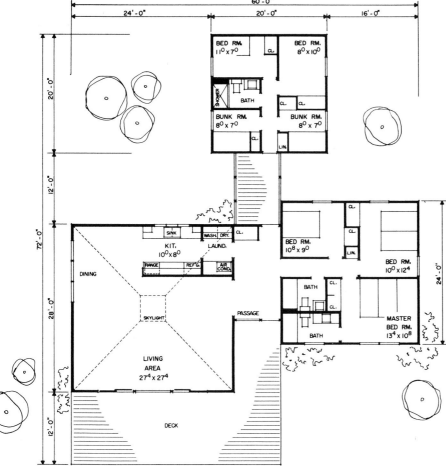

Design 52453 *1,888 Sq. Ft.; 19,908 Cu. Ft.*

● This T-shaped cluster takes a large, 28 foot square living-dining-kitchen (2828-LDK) unit and gives it two sleeping unit companions – a 24 foot square three bedroom unit (2424-3 BR) and a 20 foot square four bedroom unit (2020-4 BR). Without any problem at all you'll be able to sleep an even dozen of your friends and family members. When it comes time to eat, the dining area provides plenty of space for the whole gang. As for just plain relaxation, you'll choose between the big living area with sloping skylighted ceiling, and the sweeping outdoor deck. Two pairs of sliding glass doors allow for plenty of natural light and easy access between the indoor and the outdoor living areas. Be sure not to overlook the private bath of the master bedroom and the separate laundry.

DESIGN YOUR OWN CLUSTER—
HERE IS THE INVENTORY OF INDIVIDUAL UNITS

2020 UNITS
20' X 20'
400 Sq. Ft.; 4,100 Cu. Ft.

DESIGN 2020-LDK
LIVING-DINING AND
KITCHEN UNIT

2424 UNITS
24' x 24'
576 Sq. Ft.; 6,106 Cu. Ft.

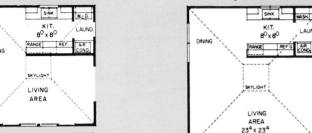

DESIGN 2424-LDK
LIVING-DINING AND
KITCHEN UNIT

2828 UNITS
28' x 28'
784 Sq. Ft.; 8,576 Cu. Ft.

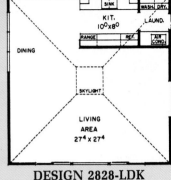

DESIGN 2828-LDK
LIVING-DINING, KITCHEN

DESIGN 2020-3 BR
3 BEDROOMS AND
BATH UNIT

DESIGN 2424-3 BR
3 BEDROOMS AND
2 BATHS UNIT

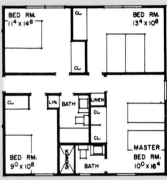

DESIGN 2828-4 BR
4 BEDROOMS, 2 BATHS

DESIGN 2020-4 BR
4 BEDROOMS AND
BATH UNIT

DESIGN 2424-4 BR
4 BEDROOMS AND
BATH UNIT

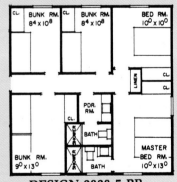

DESIGN 2828-5 BR
5 BEDROOMS, 2 BATHS

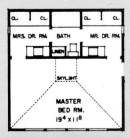

DESIGN 2020-MBR
MASTER BEDROOM
AND BATH UNIT

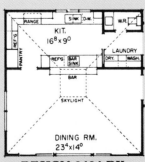

DESIGN 2424-DK
DINING, KITCHEN AND
LAUNDRY UNIT

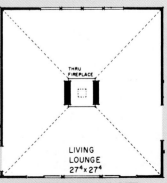

DESIGN 2828-LOFP
LOUNGE-FIREPLACE

STARTER UNITS
SIZES VARY

DESIGN 2222-LKBR*
22' x 22'
484 Sq. Ft.; 5,040 Cu. Ft.

DESIGN 2424-LKBR*
24' x 24'
576 Sq. Ft.; 6,106 Cu. Ft.

DESIGN 2626-LKBR*
26' x 26'
676 Sq. Ft.; 7,270 Cu. Ft.

DESIGN 2828-LKBR*
28' x 28'
784 Sq. Ft.; 8,576 Cu. Ft.
*LIVING-DINING,
KITCHEN, BEDROOM
AND BATH UNIT

GARAGE UNITS
SIZES VARY

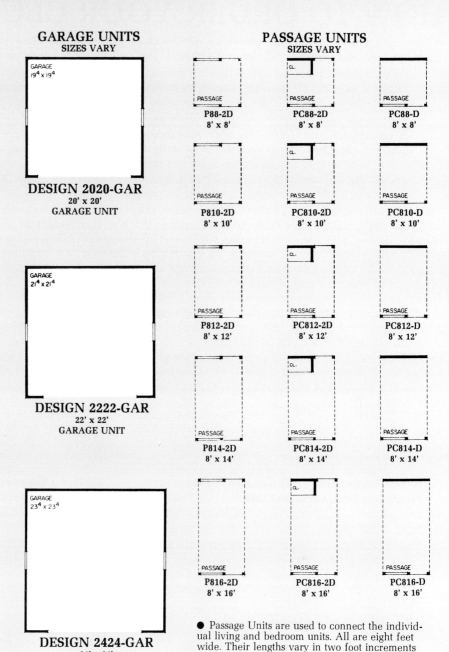

DESIGN 2020-GAR
20' x 20'
GARAGE UNIT

DESIGN 2222-GAR
22' x 22'
GARAGE UNIT

DESIGN 2424-GAR
24' x 24'
GARAGE UNIT

PASSAGE UNITS
SIZES VARY

P88-2D
8' x 8'

PC88-2D
8' x 8'

PC88-D
8' x 8'

P810-2D
8' x 10'

PC810-2D
8' x 10'

PC810-D
8' x 10'

P812-2D
8' x 12'

PC812-2D
8' x 12'

PC812-D
8' x 12'

P814-2D
8' x 14'

PC814-2D
8' x 14'

PC814-D
8' x 14'

P816-2D
8' x 16'

PC816-2D
8' x 16'

PC816-D
8' x 16'

● Passage Units are used to connect the individual living and bedroom units. All are eight feet wide. Their lengths vary in two foot increments from eight to sixteen feet. As shown above, some passage units have two doors; others one. Also, some units contain a handy closet. The walls of the adjacent cluster units automatically enclose the sides of passage units. Each order for blueprints for any individual living unit or bedroom unit includes complete construction details for all fifteen passage units.

● Here, on these two pages, are nineteen basic individual CLUSTER UNITS and fifteen sizes of connecting PASSAGE UNITS from which virtually any number of cluster designs may be planned. On the preceding pages, we have created twelve combinations with design numbers to illustrate the exciting cluster design story. Let your family and friends in on the fun of designing their own cluster. There can be many enjoyable hours spent in working out your own combinations of these versatile units. You will find it possible to satisfy even the most unique living requirements.

Remember, when tailoring your cluster to fit your building budget, you always have the option of constructing only those individual units you can afford now and then finishing at a later date. Also, clusters permit you to add livability to your grouping as the years pass and your family and your requirements grow larger.

ARCHITECTURAL PLANS AVAILABLE FOR ALL THESE INDIVIDUAL CLUSTER UNITS

HOW TO ORDER YOUR CLUSTER PLANS

● Construction blueprints can be ordered for any one of 31 different plans. These plans fall into two categories — (1) Pre-Planned Cluster Designs, and (2) Individual Cluster Units. Each category has its own price for blueprints.

-I. *Pre-Planned Cluster Designs* - There are twelve completely integrated two, three and four unit clusters offering total livability. These are clusters we have designed from the individual units shown on the inventory pages. These twelve designs are illustrated on prior pages. Blueprint prices for each of these twelve designs are $110.00 per single set; $25.00 for each additional set of same design in same order.

-II. *Individual Cluster Units* - There are nineteen separate units which comprise the basic cluster design inventory - see inventory pages. From these units it is possible to create your own "cluster." You may wish to begin with one of the starter units, and plan for the addition of any number of individual units at a later date. Blueprint prices for each of these nineteen individual cluster units, including all passage unit details, are $55.00 per single set; $25.00 for each additional set of same design in same order.

TO ORDER BLUEPRINTS . . . of the Cluster Units of your choice, merely complete the order coupon below and mail with your remittance to Home Planners, Inc. However, if it is not convenient for you to send a check or money order, merely indicate C.O.D. shipment. Postman will collect all charges, including postage and C.O.D. fee. C.O.D. not permitted to Canada or foreign countries. Should time be of essence, as it sometimes is with many of our customers, your telephone order will be processed the same day and shipped in the next day's mail. Simply call toll free 1-800-521-6797 (Michigan residents call collect 0-313-477-1854).

OUR SERVICE . . . Home Planners makes every effort to process and ship each order for blueprints the same day it is received. Because of this, we have deemed it unnecessary to acknowledge receipt of our customers' orders. See order coupon below for the postage and handling charges for surface mail, air mail and foreign mail.

A NOTE REGARDING REVERSE BLUEPRINTS . . . As a special service to those wishing to build in reverse of the plan as shown, we do include an extra set of reversed blueprints for only $25.00 additional with each order. Even though the lettering and dimensions appear backward on reversed blueprints, they make a handy reference because they show the house just as it's being built in reverse from the standard blueprints - thereby helping you visualize the home better.

OUR EXCHANGE POLICY . . . Since blueprints are printed up in specific response to your individual order, we cannot honor requests for refunds. However, the first set of blueprints in any order (or the one set in a single set order) for a given design may be exchanged for a set of another design at a fee of $20.00 plus $3.00 for postage and handling via surface mail; $4.00 via air mail.

To: **Home Planners, Inc., 23761 Research Drive**
    Farmington Hills, Michigan 48204

Please rush me _____set(s) of blueprints for each of the following designs. I have circled the designs of my choice:

Pre-Planned Cluster Designs @ **$110.00 per single set; $25.00 for each additional set of the same design-**

4 Set Package of Same Design, $165.00 (Save $20.00)
7 Set Package of Same Design, $195.00 (Save $65.00)
2440, 2442, 2444, 2445, 2446, 2447
2448, 2449, 2450, 2451, 2452, 2453 $_____

Individual Cluster Unit Designs @ **$55.00 per single set; $25.00 for each additional set of the same design-**

2020-LDK	2424-3 BR	2828-5 BR	2828-LKBR
2020-3 BR	2424-4 BR	2828-LOFP	2020-GAR
2020-4 BR	2424-DK	2222-LKBR	2222-GAR
2020-MBR	2828-LDK	2424-LKBR	2424-GAR
2424-LDK	2828-4 BR	2626-LKBR	$_____

Michigan Residents add 4% sales tax $_____

FOR POSTAGE AND HANDLING CHECK & REMIT
☐ $3.00 Added to Order for Surface Mail (UPS) – Any Mdse.
☐ $4.00 Added for Priority Mail of One-Three Sets of Blueprints.
☐ $6.00 Added for Priority Mail of Four or more Sets of Blueprints.
☐ For Canadian orders add $2.00 to above applicable rates.

☐ C.O.D. PAY POSTMAN   TOTAL $_____
   (C.O.D. Within U.S.A. Only)

Name _____

Street _____

City _____ State _____ Zip _____

CREDIT CARD ORDERS ONLY: Fill in the boxes below

Credit
Card No. ☐☐☐☐☐☐☐☐☐☐☐☐☐☐☐☐

Expiration Date ☐☐ ☐☐   CHECK ONE: ☐ VISA ☐ MasterCard
Month/Year

NCV5BP   Your Signature

To: **Home Planners, Inc., 23761 Research Drive**
    Farmington Hills, Michigan 48204

Please rush me _____set(s) of blueprints for each of the following designs. I have circled the designs of my choice:

Pre-Planned Cluster Designs @ **$110.00 per single set; $25.00 for each additional set of the same design-**

4 Set Package of Same Design, $165.00 (Save $20.00)
7 Set Package of Same Design, $195.00 (Save $65.00)
2440, 2442, 2444, 2445, 2446, 2447
2448, 2449, 2450, 2451, 2452, 2453 $_____

Individual Cluster Unit Designs @ **$55.00 per single set; $25.00 for each additional set of the same design-**

2020-LDK	2424-3 BR	2828-5 BR	2828-LKBR
2020-3 BR	2424-4 BR	2828-LOFP	2020-GAR
2020-4 BR	2424-DK	2222-LKBR	2222-GAR
2020-MBR	2828-LDK	2424-LKBR	2424-GAR
2424-LDK	2828-4 BR	2626-LKBR	$_____

Michigan Residents add 4% sales tax $_____

FOR POSTAGE AND HANDLING CHECK & REMIT
☐ $3.00 Added to Order for Surface Mail (UPS) – Any Mdse.
☐ $4.00 Added for Priority Mail of One-Three Sets of Blueprints.
☐ $6.00 Added for Priority Mail of Four or more Sets of Blueprints.
☐ For Canadian orders add $2.00 to above applicable rates.

☐ C.O.D. PAY POSTMAN   TOTAL $_____
   (C.O.D. Within U.S.A. Only)

Name _____

Street _____

City _____ State _____ Zip _____

CREDIT CARD ORDERS ONLY: Fill in the boxes below

Credit
Card No. ☐☐☐☐☐☐☐☐☐☐☐☐☐☐☐☐

Expiration Date ☐☐ ☐☐   CHECK ONE: ☐ VISA ☐
Month/Year

NCV5BP   Your Signature

SECOND HOMES . . .

for the low budget. Here is an interesting representation of small houses which, because of their modest size, lend themselves for consideration as vacation homes. However, what is of significance in many cases is the contrast between the nature of these floor plans and those which have been designed specifically for leisure living. Notice how these more conventional floor plans and elevations offer more formal living patterns. Also note the more restrained use of open planning and glass. And, of course, the design of their exterior is more conventional. However, there are many who may prefer these small, more orthodox, designs as their second homes. What is your preference?

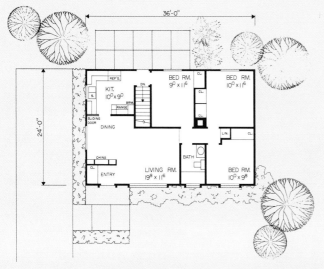

Design 52167
864 Sq. Ft.; 16,554 Cu. Ft.

● This 36' x 24' contemporary rectangle will be economical to build whether you construct the basement design at left, 52167, or the non-basement version below, 52168.

Design 52168
864 Sq. Ft.; 9,244 Cu. Ft.

● This non-basement design features a storage room and a laundry area with cupboards above the washer and dryer. Notice the space in the kitchen for eating.

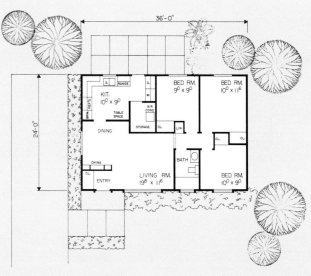

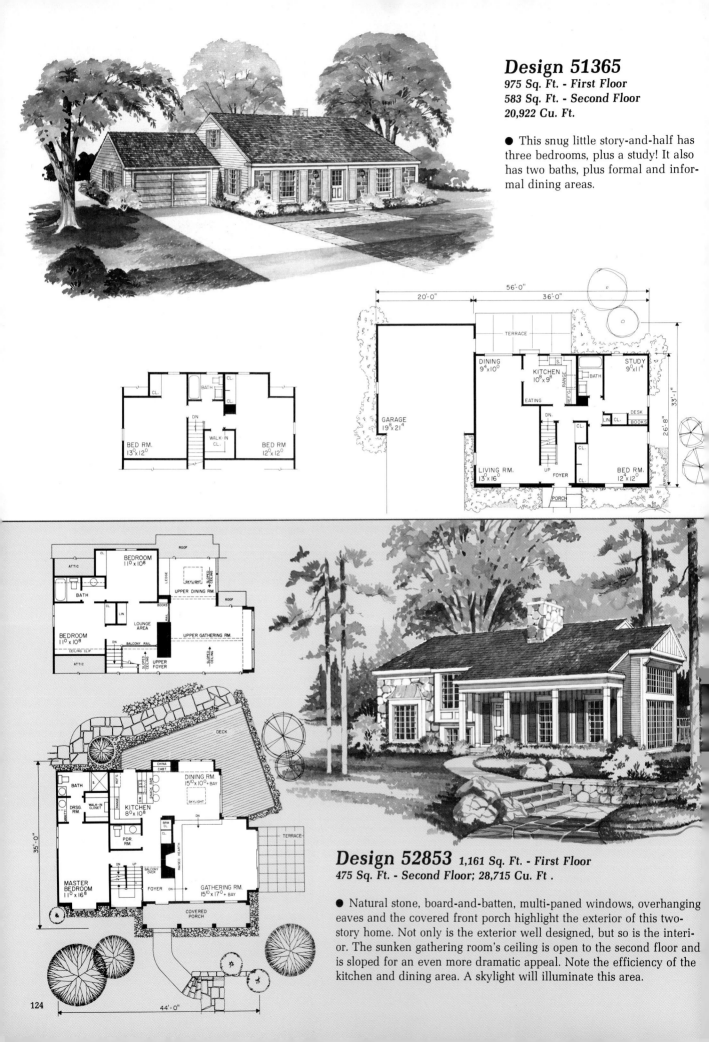

Design 51365
975 Sq. Ft. - *First Floor*
583 Sq. Ft. - *Second Floor*
20,922 Cu. Ft.

● This snug little story-and-half has three bedrooms, plus a study! It also has two baths, plus formal and informal dining areas.

BED RM. $13^0 \times 12^0$

WALK-IN CL.

BED RM. $12^0 \times 12^0$

CL.

BATH

CL.

DN

56'-0"

20'-0" 36'-0"

TERRACE

DINING $9^4 \times 10^0$

KITCHEN $10^8 \times 9^8$

S.

RANGE

REF. G.

BATH

STUDY $9^0 \times 11^4$

EATING

LIN. CL.

DESK BOOKS

33'-1"

26'-8"

DN.

CL.

GARAGE $19^4 \times 21^4$

LIVING RM. $13^0 \times 16^0$

UP

FOYER

CL.

CL.

BED RM. $12^4 \times 12^0$

PORCH

Design 52853
1,161 Sq. Ft. - *First Floor*
475 Sq. Ft. - *Second Floor*; 28,715 Cu. Ft .

● Natural stone, board-and-batten, multi-paned windows, overhanging eaves and the covered front porch highlight the exterior of this two-story home. Not only is the exterior well designed, but so is the interior. The sunken gathering room's ceiling is open to the second floor and is sloped for an even more dramatic appeal. Note the efficiency of the kitchen and dining area. A skylight will illuminate this area.

ATTIC

CL.

BEDROOM $11^0 \times 10^8$

ROOF

BATH

LEDGE

SKYLIGHT

SLOPED CEILING

UPPER DINING RM.

CL. LIN

BOOKS

ROOF

BEDROOM $11^0 \times 10^8$

LOUNGE AREA

RAIL

UPPER GATHERING RM.

DN

BALCONY RAIL

SLOPED CEILING

UPPER FOYER

SLOPED CEILING

CEILING CLIP

ATTIC

DECK

BATH

S.

REF.G.

CHINA CABT

SNACK BAR

DINING RM. $15^{10} \times 10^0$ + BAY

DRSG. RM.

WALK-IN CLOSET

KITCHEN $8^0 \times 10^8$

SKYLIGHT

VANITY

PDR. RM.

BRM CL.

CL.

DN

35'-0"

MASTER BEDROOM $11^0 \times 16^8$

DN UP

BALCONY OVER

RAISED HEARTH

FOYER

GATHERING RM. $15^{10} \times 17^0$ + BAY

COVERED PORCH

TERRACE

44'-0"

Contents

Design 51354

644 Sq. Ft. - First Floor
572 Sq. Ft. - Second Floor
11,490 Cu. Ft.

● Livability galore for the 50 foot building site. The homemaker will enjoy the U-shaped work center with the extra washroom, laundry equipment nearby.

OPTIONAL BASEMENT

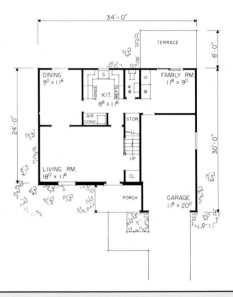

Design 51913

740 Sq. Ft. - First Floor
728 Sq. Ft. - Second Floor
20,860 Cu. Ft.

● With or without a basement this will be a great low-cost two-story home for the large family. Note first floor laundry, washroom.

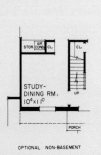

OPTIONAL NON-BASEMENT

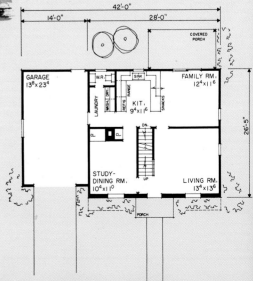

Design 51723

888 Sq. Ft. - First Floor
970 Sq. Ft. - Second Floor
19,089 Cu. Ft.

● You'll not need a large parcel of property to accommodate this home. Neither will you need too large a building budget. Note fourth bedroom.

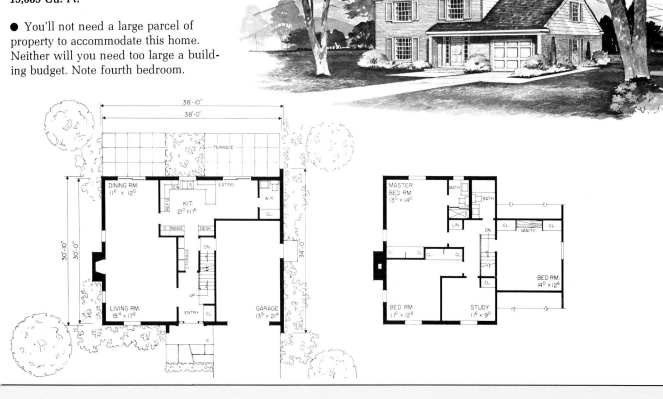

Design 51368

728 Sq. Ft. - First Floor
728 Sq. Ft. - Second Floor
20,020 Cu. Ft.

● Similar in plan to 51913 on the opposing page, this home features an entirely different exterior. Which do you prefer? Note covered rear porches.

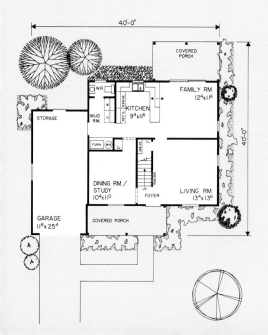

Design 52657

1,217 Sq. Ft. - First Floor
868 Sq. Ft. - Second Floor
33,260 Cu. Ft.

● Deriving its design from the traditional Cape Cod style, this facade features clap board siding, small-paned windows and a transom-lit entrance flanked by carriage lamps. A central chimney services two fireplaces, one in the country-kitchen and the other in the formal living room which is removed from the disturbing flow of traffic. The master suite is located to the left of the upstairs landing. A full bathroom services two additional bedrooms.

● Traditional charm of yesteryear is exemplified delightfully in this one-and-a-half story home. The garage has been conveniently tucked away in the rear of the house which makes this design ideal for a corner lot. Interior livability has been planned for efficient living. The front living room is large and features a fireplace with wood box.

Design 52658

1,218 Sq. Ft. - First Floor
764 Sq. Ft. - Second Floor
29,690 Cu. Ft.

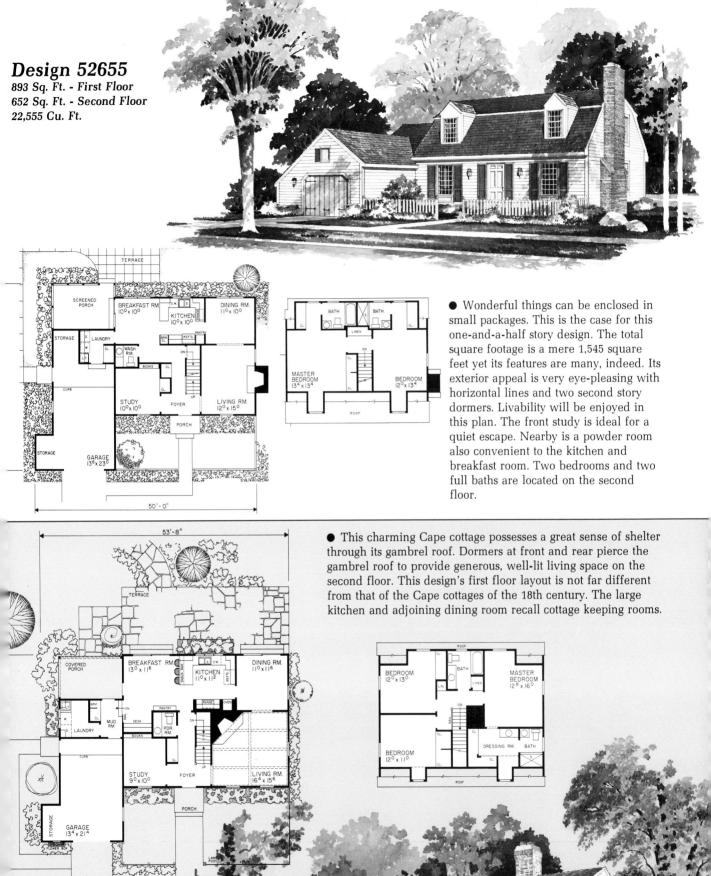

Design 52655
893 Sq. Ft. - First Floor
652 Sq. Ft. - Second Floor
22,555 Cu. Ft.

TERRACE

SCREENED PORCH

BREAKFAST RM. 10⁰ x 10⁰

KITCHEN 10⁰ x 10⁰

DINING RM. 11⁰ x 10⁰

STORAGE

LAUNDRY

WASH RM.

PANTRY

REF'G

BOOKS

STUDY 10⁰ x 10⁰

FOYER

UP

LIVING RM. 12⁰ x 15⁰

PORCH

CURB

STORAGE

GARAGE 13⁸ x 23⁰

50'-0"

BATH LINEN BATH

MASTER BEDROOM 13⁴ x 13⁴

DN

BEDROOM 12⁰ x 13⁴

ROOF

● Wonderful things can be enclosed in small packages. This is the case for this one-and-a-half story design. The total square footage is a mere 1,545 square feet yet its features are many, indeed. Its exterior appeal is very eye-pleasing with horizontal lines and two second story dormers. Livability will be enjoyed in this plan. The front study is ideal for a quiet escape. Nearby is a powder room also convenient to the kitchen and breakfast room. Two bedrooms and two full baths are located on the second floor.

● This charming Cape cottage possesses a great sense of shelter through its gambrel roof. Dormers at front and rear pierce the gambrel roof to provide generous, well-lit living space on the second floor. This design's first floor layout is not far different from that of the Cape cottages of the 18th century. The large kitchen and adjoining dining room recall cottage keeping rooms.

53'-8"

TERRACE

COVERED PORCH

BREAKFAST RM. 13⁰ x 11⁶

KITCHEN 11⁰ x 11²

DINING RM. 11⁰ x 11⁶

LAUNDRY

MUD RM.

DESK

PANTRY

POR. RM.

BOOKS

RANGE OVEN

FOYER

UP

DN

STUDY 9⁰ x 10⁰

LIVING RM. 16⁴ x 15⁶

CURB

PORCH

GARAGE 13⁴ x 21⁴

STORAGE

FLOWER BOX

LAMP POST

BEDROOM 12⁰ x 13⁰

BATH

LINEN

MASTER BEDROOM 12⁸ x 16⁰

ROOF

DN

BEDROOM 12⁰ x 11⁰

DRESSING RM.

BATH

ROOF

Design 52656
1,122 Sq. Ft. - First Floor
884 Sq. Ft. - Second Floor
31,845 Cu. Ft.

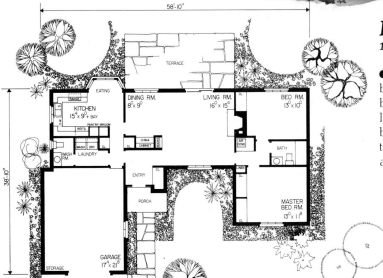

Design 52607
1,208 Sq. Ft.; 25,622 Cu. Ft.

● Here is an English Tudor retirement cottage. Its by-word is "convenience". There are two sizable bedrooms, a full bath, plus an extra wash room. The living and dining areas are spacious and overlook both front and rear yards. Sliding glass doors lead to the outdoor terrace. In addition to the formal dining area with its built-in china cabinet, there is a delightful breakfast eating alcove in the kitchen. The U-shaped work area is wonderfully efficient, and around the corner is the laundry. Blueprints include optional basement details.

Design 52570
1,176 Sq. Ft.; 26,800 Cu. Ft.

● This attractive Tudor is another economically built design which will cater admirably to the living patterns of the retired couple. In addition to the two bedrooms this plan offers a study which could double ideally as a guest room, sewing room or even serve as the TV room. The living area is a spacious L-shaped zone for formal living and dining. The efficient kitchen is handy to the front door and overlooks the front yard. It features a convenient breakfast nook for those informal meals.

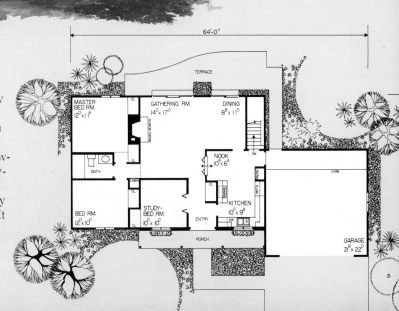

130

All The "TOOLS" You And Your Builder Need

. . to, first select an exterior and a floor plan for your new house that satisfy your tastes and your family's living patterns . . .

. . then, to review the blueprints in great detail and obtain a construction cost figure . . . also, to price out the structural materials required to build . . . and, finally, to review and decide upon the specifications to which your home is to be built. Truly, an invaluable set of "tools" to launch your home planning and building programs.

. THE PLAN BOOKS

Home Planners' unique Design Category Series makes it easy to look at and study only the types of designs for which you and your family have an interest. Each of six plan books features a specific type of home, namely: Two-Story, 1½ Story, One-Story Over 2000 Sq. Ft., One-Story Under 2000 Sq. Ft., Multi-Levels and Vacation Homes. In addition to the convenient Design Category Series, there is an impressive selection of other current titles. While the home plans featured in these books are also to be found in the Design Category Series, they, too, are edited for those with special tastes and requirements. Your family will spend many enjoyable hours reviewing the delightfully designed exteriors and the practical floor plans. Surely your home or office library should include a selection of these popular plan books. Your complete satisfaction is guaranteed.

. THE CONSTRUCTION BLUEPRINTS

There are blueprints available for each of the designs published in Home Planners' current plan books. Depending upon the size, the style and the type of home, each set of blueprints consists of from five to ten large sheets. Only by studying the blueprints is it possible to give complete and final consideration to the proper selection of a design for your next home. The blueprints provide the opportunity for all family members to familiarize themselves with the features of all exterior elevations, interior elevations and details, all dimensions, special built-in features and effects. They also provide a full understanding of the materials to be used and/or selected. The low-cost of our blueprints makes it possible and indeed, practical, to study in detail a number of different sets of blueprints before deciding upon which design to build.

3. THE MATERIALS LIST
A list of materials is an integral part of the plan package. It comprises the last sheet of each set of blueprints and serves as a handy reference during the period of construction. Of course, at the pricing and the material ordering stages, it is indispensable.

4. THE SPECIFICATION OUTLINE
Each order for blueprints is accompanied by one Specification Outline. You and your builder will find this a time-saving tool when deciding upon your own individual specifications. An important reference document should you wish to write your own specifications.

The Design Category Series

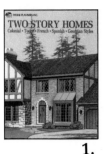

1.

360 TWO STORY HOMES

English Tudors, Early American Salt Boxes, Gambrels, Farmhouses, Southern Colonials, Georgians, French Mansards, Contemporaries. Interesting floor plans for both small and large families. Efficient kitchens, 2 to 6 bedrooms, family rooms, libraries, extra baths, mud rooms. Homes for all budgets.

288 Pages, $6.95

2.

150 1½ STORY HOMES

Cape Cod, Williamsburg, Georgian, Tudor and Contemporary versions. Low budget and country-estate feature sections. Expandable family plans. Formal and informal living and dining areas along with gathering rooms. Spacious, country kitchens. Indoor-outdoor livability with covered porches and functional terraces.

128 Pages, $3.95

3.

210 ONE STORY HO OVER 2,000 Sq. Ft.

All popular styles. Inc Spanish, Western, French, and other trad versions. Contempo Gracious, family livin terns. Sunken living master bedroom suite ums, courtyards, pools indoor-outdoor living tionships. For mod country-estate budgets.

192 Pages, $4.95

4.

315 ONE STORY HOMES UNDER 2,000 Sq. Ft.

A great selection of traditional and contemporary exteriors for medium and restricted budgets. Efficient, practical floor plans. Gathering rooms, formal and informal living and dining rooms, mud rooms, indoor-outdoor livability. Economically built homes. Designs with bonus space livability for growing families.

192 Pages, $4.95

5.

215 MULTI-LEVEL HOMES

For new dimensions in family living. A captivating variety of exterior styles, exciting floor plans for flat and sloping sites. Exposed lower levels. Balconies, decks. Plans for the active family. Upper level lounges, excellent bath facilities. Sloping ceilings. Functional outdoor terraces. For all building budgets.

192 Pages, $4.95

6.

223 VACATION HO

Features A-Frames, Hexagons, economical gles. One and two stori multi-levels. Lodges fr 'round livability. From 3238 sq. ft. Cottages sle to 22. For flat or slopi Spacious, open plannin 600 illustrations. 120 P full color. Cluster selection. For lakesh woodland leisure living.

176 Pages, $4.95

The Exterior Style Series

7.

330 EARLY AMERICAN PLANS

Our new *Essential Guide to Early American Home Plans* traces Early American architecture from our Colonial Past to Traditional styles popular today with a written history of designs and colorful sections devoted to styles. Many of our designs are patterned after historic homes.

304 Pages, $9.95

8.

335 CONTEMPORARY HOME PLANS

Our new *Essential Guide to Contemporary Home Plans* offers a colorful directory to modern architecture, including a history of American Contemporary styling and more than 335 home plans of all sizes and popular designs. 304 colorful pages!

304 Pages, $9.95

9.

135 ENGLISH TUD HOMES

and other Popular Plans is a favorite of The current popularity English Tudor home d phenomenal. Here is which is loaded with for all budgets. The one-story, 1½ and tw designs, plus multi-lev hillsides from 1,176 to ft. There is a special section of Early A Adaptations.

104 Pages, $3.95

The Budget Series

13.

175 LOW BUDGET HOMES

A special selection of home designs for the modest or restricted building budget. An excellent variety of Traditional and Contemporary designs. One-story, 1½ and two-story and split-level homes. Three, four and five bedrooms. Family rooms, extra baths, formal and informal dining rooms. Basement and non-basement designs. Attached garages an covered porches.

96 Pages, $2.95

14.

165 AFFORDABLE HOME PLANS

This outstanding book was specially edited with a wide selection of houses and plans for those with a medium building budget. While none of these designs are considered low-cost; neither do they require an unlimited budget to build. Square footages range from 1,428. Exteriors of Tudor, French, Early American, Spanish and Contemporary are included.

112 Pages, $2.95

15.

142 HOME DESIG FOR EXPANDED BUILDING BUDGE

A family's ability to and need for a larg grows as its size and increases. This selecti lights designs which h average square foo 2,551. One-story plans 2,069; two-stories, multi-levels, 2,825. homes featuring raise fireplaces, open plan efficient kitchens.

112 Pages, $2.95

The Full Color Series

116 TRADITIONAL and CONTEMPORARY PLANS

A beautifully illustrated home plan book in complete, full color. One, 1½, two-story and split-level designs featured in all of the most popular exterior styles. Varied building budgets will be satisfied by the numerous plans for all budget sizes. Designs for flat and hillside sites, including exposed lower levels. It will make an ideal gift item.

17.

96 Pages in Full Color, $5.95

122 HOME DESIGNS

This book has full color throughout. More than 120 eye-pleasing, colored illustrations. Tudor, French, Spanish, Early American and Contemporary exteriors featuring all design types. The interiors house efficient, step-saving floor plans. Formal and informal living areas along with convenient work centers. Two to six bedroom sleeping areas. A delightful book for one's permanent library.

18.

96 Pages in Full Color, $5.95

114 TREND HOMES

Heritage Houses, Energy Designs, Family Plans - these, along with Vacation Homes, are in this new plan book in full color. The Trend Homes feature unique living patterns. The revered Heritage Houses highlight the charm and nostalgia of Early America. Solariums, greenhouses, earth-sheltered and super-insulated houses are the Energy Designs. Vacation homes feature A-frames and chalets.

19.

104 Pages in Full Color, $5.95

450 HOUSE PLANS

For those who wish to review and study perhaps the largest selection of designs available in a single volume. This edition will provide countless hours of enjoyable family home planning. Varying exterior styles, plus interesting and practical floor plans for all building budgets. Formal, informal living patterns; indoor-outdoor livability; small, growing and large family facilities.

23.

320 Pages, $9.95

136 SPANISH & WESTERN HOME DESIGNS

Stucco exteriors, arches, tile roofs, wide-overhangs, courtyards and rambling ranches are characteristics which make this design selection distinctive. These sun-country designs highlight indoor-outdoor relationships. Solar oriented livability is featured. Their appeal is not limited to the Southwest region of our country.

10.

120 Pages, $2.95

The Plan Books

. . are a most valuable tool for anyone planning to build a new home. A study of the hundreds of delightfully designed exteriors and the practical, efficient floor plans will be a great learning and fun-oriented family experience. You will be able to select your preferred styling from among Early American, Tudor, French, Spanish and Contemporary adaptations. Your ideas about floor planning and interior livability will expand. And, of course, after you have selected an appealing home design that satisfies your long list of living requirements, you can order the blueprints for further study of your favorite design in greater detail. Surely the hours spent studying the portfolio of Home Planners' designs will be both enjoyable and rewarding ones.

Frontal Sheet

Detailed Floor Plans

Foundation Plans

House Cross-Sections

Interior Elevations

Exterior Elevations

Material List

The Blueprints

1. FRONTAL SHEET.
Artist's landscaped sketch of the exterior and ink-line floor plans are on the frontal sheet of each set of blueprints.

2. FOUNDATION PLAN.
¼" Scale basement and foundation plan. All necessary notations and dimensions. Plot plan diagram for locating house on building site.

3. DETAILED FLOOR PLAN.
¼" Scale first and second floor plans with complete dimensions. Cross-section detail keys. Diagrammatic layout of electrical outlets and switches.

4. HOUSE CROSS-SECTIONS.
Large scale sections of foundation, interior and exterior walls, floors and roof details for design and construction control.

5. INTERIOR ELEVATIONS.
Large scale interior details of the complete kitchen cabinet design, bathrooms, powder room, laundry, fireplaces, paneling, beam ceilings, built-in cabinets, etc.

6. EXTERIOR ELEVATIONS.
¼" Scale exterior elevation drawings of front, rear, and both sides of the house. All exterior materials and details are shown to indicate the complete design and proportions of the house.

7. MATERIAL LIST.
Complete lists of all materials required for the construction of the house as designed are included in each set of blueprints.

THIS BLUEPRINT PACKAGE
will help you and your family take a major step forward in the final appraisal and planning of your new home. Only by spending many enjoyable and informative hours studying the numerous details included in the complete package, will you feel sure of, and comfortable with, your commitment to build your new home. To assure successful and productive consultation with your builder and/or architect, reference to the various elements of the blueprint package is a must. The blueprints, material list and specification outline will save much consultation time and expense. Don't be without them.

The Material List

With each set of blueprints you order you will receive a material list. Each list shows you the quantity, type and size of the non-mechanical materials required to build your home. It also tells you where these materials are used. This makes the blueprints easy to understand.

Influencing the mechanical requirements are geographical differences in availability of materials, local codes, methods of installation and individual preferences. Because of these factors, your local heating, plumbing and electrical contractors can supply you with necessary material take-offs for their particular trades.

Material lists simplify your material ordering and enable you to get quicker price quotations from your builder and material dealer. Because the material list is an integral part of each set of blueprints, it is not available separately.

Among the materials listed:

• Masonry, Veneer & Fireplace • Framing Lumber • Roofing & Sheet Metal • Windows & Door Frames • Exterior Trim & Insulation • Tile Work, Finish Floors • Interior Trim, Kitchen Cabinets • Rough & Finish Hardware

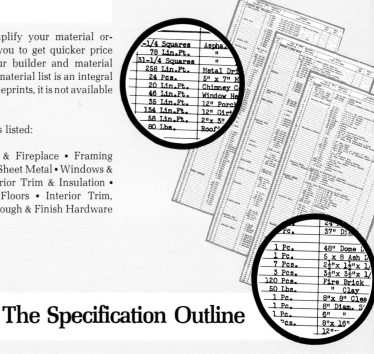

The Specification Outline

This fill-in type specification lists over 150 phases of home construction from excavating to painting and includes wiring, plumbing, heating and air-conditioning. It consists of 16 pages and will prove invaluable for specifying to your builder the exact materials, equipment and methods of construction you want in your new home. One Specification Outline is included free with each order for blueprints. Additional Specification Outlines are available at $3.00 each.

CONTENTS
• General Instructions, Suggestions and Information • Excavating and Grading • Masonry and Concrete Work • Sheet Metal Work • Carpentry, Millwork, Roofing, and Miscellaneous Items • Lath and Plaster or Drywall Wallboard • Schedule for Room Finishes • Painting and Finishing • Tile Work • Electrical Work • Plumbing • Heating and Air-Conditioning

Before You Order

1. STUDY THE DESIGNS . . . found in Home Planners current publications. As you review these delightful custom homes, you should keep in mind the total living requirements of your family – both indoors and outdoors. Although we do not make changes in plans, many minor changes can be made prior to the period of construction. If major changes are involved to satisfy your personal requirements, you should consider ordering one set of blueprints and having them redrawn locally. Consultation with your architect is strongly advised when contemplating major changes.

2. HOW TO ORDER BLUEPRINTS . . . After you have chosen the design that satisfies your requirements, or if you have selected one that you wish to study in more detail, simply clip the accompanying order blank and mail with your remittance. However, if it is not convenient for you to send a check or money order, you can use your credit card, or merely indicate C.O.D. shipment. Postman will collect all charges, including postage and C.O.D. fee. C.O.D. shipments are not permitted to Canada or foreign countries. Should time be of essence, as it sometimes is with many of our customers, your telephone order usually can be processed and shipped in the next day's mail. Simply call toll free 1-800-521-6797, (Michigan residents call collect 0-313-477-1854).

3. OUR SERVICE . . . Home Planners makes every effort to process and ship each order for blueprints and books within 48 hours. Because of this, we have deemed it unnecessary to acknowledge receipt of our customers orders. See order coupon for the postage and handling charges for surface mail, air mail or foreign mail.

4. A NOTE REGARDING REVERSE BLUE-PRINTS . . . As a special service to those wishing to build in reverse of the plan as shown, we do include an extra set of reversed blueprints for only $25.00 additional with each order. Even though the lettering and dimensions appear backward on reversed blueprints, they make a handy reference because they show the house just as it's being built in reverse from the standard blueprints — thereby helping you visualize the home better.

5. OUR EXCHANGE POLICY . . . Since blueprints are printed up in specific response to your individual order, we cannot honor requests for refunds. However, the first set of blueprints in any order (or the one set in a single set order) for a given design may be exchanged for a set of another design at a fee of $20.00 plus $3.00 for postage and handling via surface mail; $4.00 via air mail.

TO: HOME PLANNERS, INC., 23761 RESEARCH DRIVE FARMINGTON HILLS, MICHIGAN 48024

Please rush me the following:

____ SET(S) BLUEPRINTS FOR DESIGN NO(S). _____ $_____
  Single Set, $110.00; Additional Identical Sets in Same Order $25.00 ea.
  4 Set Package of Same Design, $165.00 (Save $20.00)
  7 Set Package of Same Design, $195.00 (Save $65.00)
  (Material Lists and 1 Specification Outline included)
____ SPECIFICATION OUTLINES @ $3.00 EACH . . . . $_____

Michigan Residents add 4% sales tax $_____

FOR POSTAGE ☐ $3.00 Added to Order for Surface Mail (UPS) – Any Mdse.
AND HANDLING ☐ $4.00 Added for Priority Mail of One-Three Sets of Blueprints.
PLEASE CHECK ☐ $6.00 Added for Priority Mail of Four or more Sets of Blueprints. } $_____
✔ & REMIT ☐ For Canadian orders add $2.00 to above applicable rates

☐ C.O.D. PAY POSTMAN
(C.O.D. Within U.S.A. Only)   TOTAL in U.S.A. funds $_____

PLEASE PRINT
Name _____
Street _____
City _____ State _____ Zip _____

CREDIT CARD ORDERS ONLY: Fill in the boxes below   Prices subject to change without notice
Credit Card No. ☐☐☐☐☐☐☐☐☐☐☐☐☐☐☐☐   Expiration Date Month/Year ☐☐☐☐

CHECK ONE: ☐ VISA® ☐ MasterCard   Your Signature _____

Order Form Key NCV5BP

BLUEPRINT ORDERS SHIPPED WITHIN 48 HOURS OF RECEIPT!

TO: HOME PLANNERS, INC., 23761 RESEARCH DRIVE FARMINGTON HILLS, MICHIGAN 48024

Please rush me the following:

____ SET(S) BLUEPRINTS FOR DESIGN NO(S). _____ $_____
  Single Set, $110.00; Additional Identical Sets in Same Order $25.00 ea.
  4 Set Package of Same Design, $165.00 (Save $20.00)
  7 Set Package of Same Design, $195.00 (Save $65.00)
  (Material Lists and 1 Specification Outline included)
____ SPECIFICATION OUTLINES @ $3.00 EACH . . . . $_____

Michigan Residents add 4% sales tax $_____

FOR POSTAGE ☐ $3.00 Added to Order for Surface Mail (UPS) – Any Mdse.
AND HANDLING ☐ $4.00 Added for Priority Mail of One-Three Sets of Blueprints.
PLEASE CHECK ☐ $6.00 Added for Priority Mail of Four or more Sets of Blueprints. } $_____
✔ & REMIT ☐ For Canadian orders add $2.00 to above applicable rates

☐ C.O.D. PAY POSTMAN
(C.O.D. Within U.S.A. Only)   TOTAL in U.S.A. funds $_____

PLEASE PRINT
Name _____
Street _____
City _____ State _____ Zip _____

CREDIT CARD ORDERS ONLY: Fill in the boxes below   Prices subject to change without notice
Credit Card No. ☐☐☐☐☐☐☐☐☐☐☐☐☐☐☐☐   Expiration Date Month/Year ☐☐☐☐

CHECK ONE: ☐ VISA® ☐ MasterCard   Your Signature _____

Order Form Key NCV5BP

How many sets of blueprints should be ordered?

This question is often asked. The answer can range anywhere from 1 to 7 sets, depending upon circumstances. For instance, a single set of blueprints of your favorite design is sufficient to study the house in greater detail. On the other hand, if you are planning to get cost estimates, or if you are planning to build, you may need as many as seven sets of blueprints. Because the first set of blueprints in each order is $110.00, and because additional sets of the same design in each order are only $25.00 each (and with package sets even more economical), you save considerably by ordering your total requirements now. To help you determine the exact number of sets, please refer to the handy check list.

How Many Blueprints Do You Need?

__OWNER'S SET

__BUILDER (Usually requires at least 3 sets: 1 legal document; 1 for inspection; and at least for tradesmen — usually more.)

__BUILDING PERMIT (Sometimes 2 sets are required.)

__MORTGAGE SOURCE (Usually 1 set for conventional mortgage; 3 sets for F.H.A. or V.A. type mortgages.)

__SUBDIVISION COMMITTEE (If any.)

__TOTAL NO. SETS REQUIRED

Blueprint Ordering Hotline –

Phone toll free: 1-800-521-6797.
Orders received by 11 a.m. (Detroit time) will be processed the same day and shipped to you the following day. Use of this line restricted to blueprint ordering only. Michigan residents simply call collect 0-313-477-1854.

Kindly Note: When ordering by phone, please state Order Form Key No. located in box at lower left corner of blueprint order form.

In Canada Mail To:
Home Planners, Inc., 20 Cedar St. North Kitchener, Ontario N2H 2W8
Phone: (519) 743-4169

TWO-STORY HOMES . . .

for spacious vacation living. As with the conventional two-story home, the leisure-living two-story represents a most economical use of the construction dollar by stacking livability. As these designs show, utilizing the second floor solves that oft lamented problem of weekend vacation living - where does everybody sleep? While one may be hesitant to introduce the upstairs lounge into the primary home, the vacation home may be just the place for it. Notice its utilization and dramatic appeal in a couple of the designs in this section. For complete privacy, the featured duplex may be just the answer where two families are hesitant to share all their vacation time together.

Design 52481
1,160 Sq. Ft. - First Floor
828 Sq. Ft. - Second Floor; 18,018 Cu. Ft.

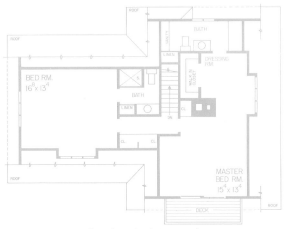

● Five rooms for sleeping! A complete master suite plus three bedrooms and a bunk room. Three full baths, one on the first floor and two upstairs. The living room will enjoy easy access to a large deck plus a fireplace. The dining room is conveniently located between the living area and the efficient kitchen which has a pantry and nearby laundry/utility room. Surely a great planned work center for a vacation home.

Design 52419

1,018 Sq. Ft. – First Floor
392 Sq. Ft. – Second Floor; 16,368 Cu. Ft.

● Dramatic appeal, are the words which aptly describe this two-story family haven. The architectural detailing which encloses a spacious interior is, indeed, refreshing. Of unusual interest are such features as the roof areas, the window treatment and the large wood deck. The sleeping potential is exceptional and will be restricted only by the number of bunk beds you decide to place in each of the four bedrooms. Observe closets.

Design 52415
976 Sq. Ft. – First Floor
480 Sq. Ft. – Second Floor; 15,830 Cu. Ft.

● Reminiscent of the lines of some of the old traditional houses, this design gets its contemporary flavor from the up-to-date window treatment. The shed roofs, the clapboard siding and the wide corner boards are the pleasing features of an earlier memorable era. As for the floor planning and resultant livability, there is nothing old fashioned here. There is a bright, cheerful interior with plenty of open space. Note bunk balcony and storage rooms.

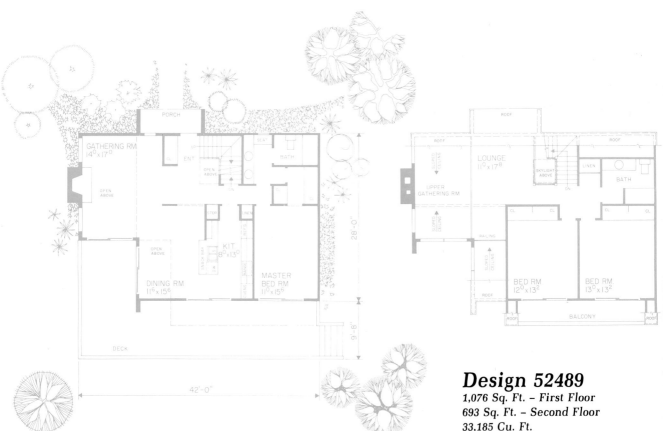

Design 52489

1,076 Sq. Ft. – First Floor
693 Sq. Ft. – Second Floor
33,185 Cu. Ft.

● Outdoors-oriented families will appreciate the dramatic sliding glass doors and the sweeping decks that make this contemporary perfect. The plan of the first floor features a spacious two-story gathering room with sloping ceiling, a large fireplace and access to the large deck which runs the full length of the house. Also having direct access to the deck is the dining room which is half-open to the second floor above. A snack bar divides the dining room from the compact kitchen The master bedroom is outstanding with its private bath, walk-in closet an sliding glass door. The second floor is brightened by a skylight and houses two bedrooms, lounge and full bath.

Design 52484
869 Sq. Ft. – First Floor
948 Sq. Ft. – Second Floor
28,560 Cu. Ft.

● A two-story leisure-time house with all the comforts of home and maybe even a few more. Yet, the enviroment, the atmosphere and the living patterns will be entirely different. Imagine the fun everybody will have during their visits to this delightfully contemporary retreat. The large glass areas preserve the view from the rear. The upstairs lounge looks down into the gathering room. There are two eating areas adjacent to the U-shaped kitchen which could hardly be more efficient. There are 2½ baths, a fireplace, an attached garage and a basement. If you wish to forego the basement, locate the heating equipment where the basement stairs and pantry are located.

Design 52474

1,163 Sq. Ft. – Main Level
989 Sq. Ft. – Upper Level
180 Sq. Ft. – Lower Level
32,380 Cu. Ft.

48'-0"
36'-0"

32'-0"

44'-0"

ROOF
ROOF
BATH
PDR. RM.
KIT.
11⁶ x 11²
LINEN
WALK-IN CL.
BOOKS BOOKS BOOKS
CABINETS
DN
DN
DN
LOWER LOUNGE
12⁰ x 18²
DINING RM.
12⁰ x 20⁰
LIVING RM.
12⁰ x 19⁴
DECK
DN

BUNK RM.
8⁴ x 9⁴
CL
BATH
MASTER BATH
LINEN
DRESS. RM.
CL
CL
BALCONY
BALCONY
BALCONY
BED RM.
8⁴ x 12⁴
MASTER BED RM.
10⁸ x 12⁰
SLOPED CEILING
SLOPED CEILING
SLOPED CEILING
SLOPED CEILING
BED RM.
9⁰ x 9⁴
UPPER LOUNGE
BED RM.
9⁶ x 9⁴

PARKING AREA
AUTO AREA
11⁰ x 30⁸
W.R.
LAUNDRY
BOAT AREA
11⁰ x 3
GAMES & STORAGE
RECREATION AREA
12⁰ x 15⁸

142

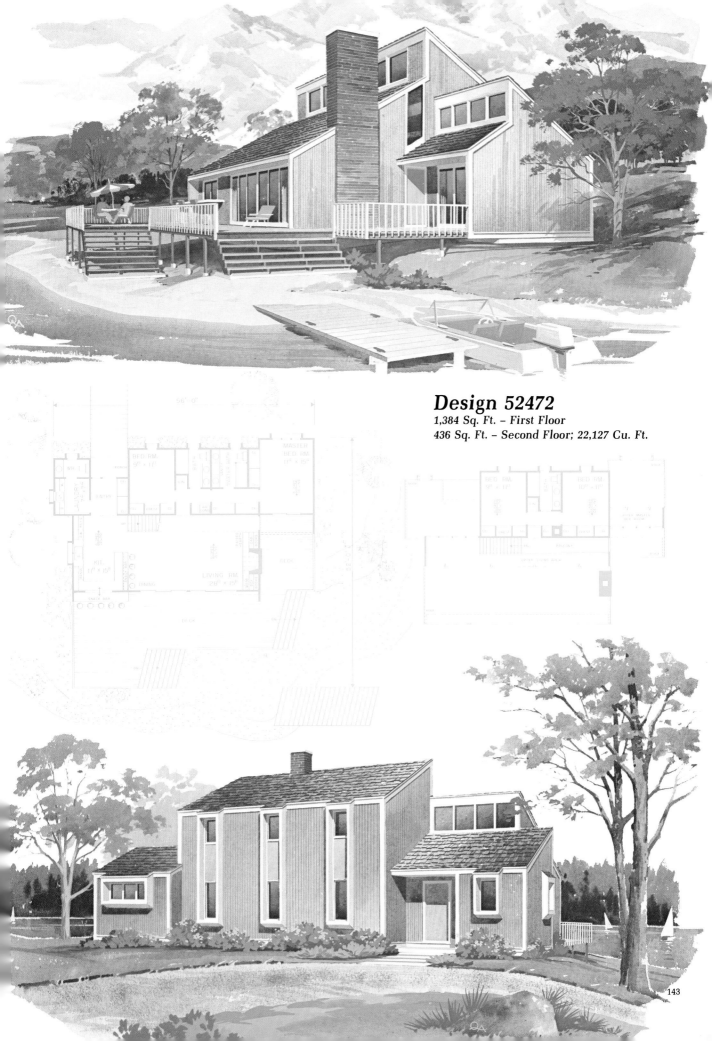

Design 52472
1,384 Sq. Ft. – First Floor
436 Sq. Ft. – Second Floor; 22,127 Cu. Ft.

143

Design 51450 *1,008 Sq. Ft. – First Floor; 476 Sq. Ft. – Second Floor; 17,570 Cu. Ft.*

● What leisure-time fun you, your family and friends will experience in this appealing and wonderfully planned design. And little wonder, for all the elements are present to guarantee vacation living patterns. Four good-sized bedrooms solve the problem of accommodating overnight weekend guests. A full bath on each floor is an important feature. In addition, there is a stall shower handy to the side entrance – just the right location to cater to the requirements of swimmers. The sweeping outdoor deck will be a favorite gathering spot. The living room is a full 27 feet long. It will be a great area to accommodate a crowd. Additional space on the screened-in porch.

Design 51464 *528 Sq. Ft. – First Floor; 272 Sq. Ft. – Second Floor; 8,045 Cu. Ft.*

● A world of care will pass you by as you and your family enjoy all that this distinctive design and its setting have to offer. The economically built floor plan offers an abundance of vacation living potential. There are three bed-

rooms, fine storage facilities and sloped ceilings. There is a strip kitchen, a full bath, an appealing balcony, a generous living area and an outdoor deck. The use of glass, as in so many vacation homes, is most interesting. While it

carries an impressive design impact it is also practical. Study its use and how your family will function during their vacation times. Any location will be a perfect backdrop for this two-story vacation design.

Design 52437
840 Sq. Ft. – First Floor
840 Sq. Ft. – Second Floor; 16,900 Cu. F

● Your living patterns as pursued in this two-story second home will leave nothing to be desired. This 20 x 40 foot rectangle delivers all the basic livability features you would demand of your year 'round domicile. As traditional as your family's living patterns will be, they will be experienced in an aura of comfort and informality. You will be constantly aware of your chosen vacation home environment. Should you have a view to be preserved, proper orientation will assure the fullest enjoyment from all major rooms in the house. Imagine the view from each of the bedrooms, the kitchen, the dining and living room. There are three baths and plenty of storage facilities.

Design 52422 1,056 Sq. Ft. – First Floor; 1,056 Sq. Ft. – Second Floor; 19,705 Cu. Ft.

● The multi-family residence does not have to be restricted to the year 'round suburban living environment. If this type of housing is sound in the city, it may be particularly so in vacationland. This design offers plenty of space for two families. The soundproof wall assures the utmost in privacy from noise of the adjoining neighbor. Each unit offers three bedrooms, 1½ baths, a huge living area, an efficient kitchen and fine storage facilities. Sliding glass doors are features of two of the upstairs bedrooms. They lead to the balcony which looks down to the lower terrace. Development of a two family outdoor living area will be lots of fun for the two families to partake.

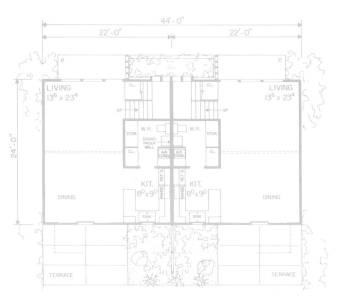

Country Style With Contemporary Living

● A country-style home is part of America's fascination with the rural past. This home's emphasis of the traditional country home is in its historic gambrel roof, dormers and fanlight windows. Having a traditional exterior from the street view, this two-story home has large window walls and a greenhouse, which opens the house to the outdoors in a thoroughly contemporary manner. The interior of this design was planned to meet the requirements of today's active family. Like the country houses of the past, this home has a large gathering room for family get-togethers or entertaining. Note its L-shape which accommodates a music alcove. This area is large enough for a grand piano and storage for TV/Stereo equipment.

Design 52883
1,919 Sq. Ft. - First Floor
895 Sq. Ft. - Second Floor; 46,489 Cu. Ft.

The adjacent two-story greenhouse doubles as the dining room. There is a pass-thru snack bar to the country kitchen here. This country kitchen just might be the heart of the house with its two areas - the work zone and the sitting room. A front study is ready for those more quiet retreats.

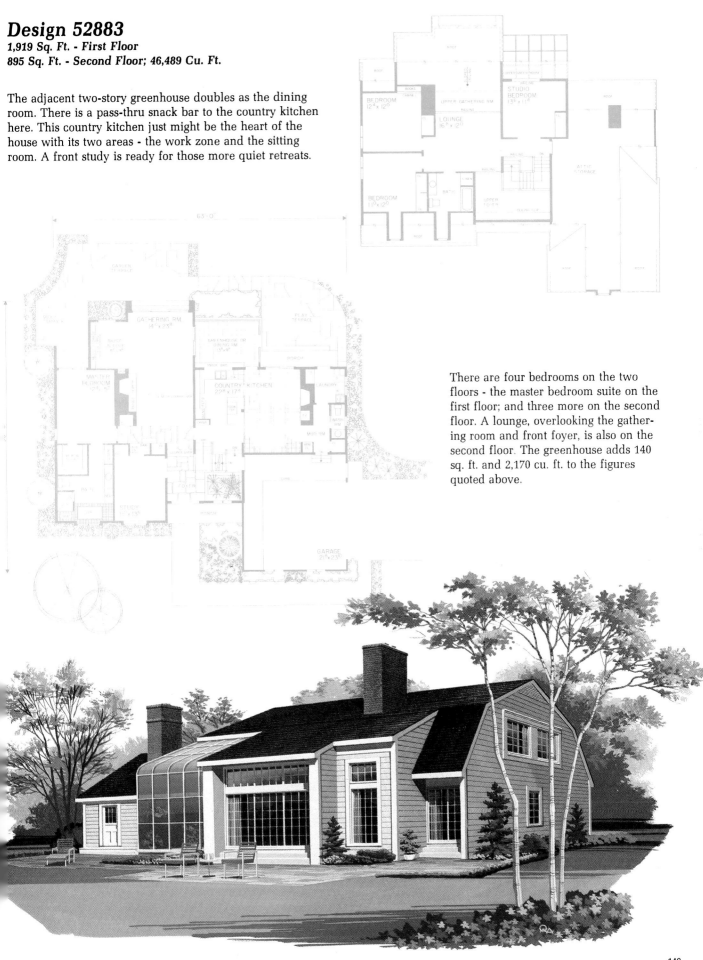

There are four bedrooms on the two floors - the master bedroom suite on the first floor; and three more on the second floor. A lounge, overlooking the gathering room and front foyer, is also on the second floor. The greenhouse adds 140 sq. ft. and 2,170 cu. ft. to the figures quoted above.

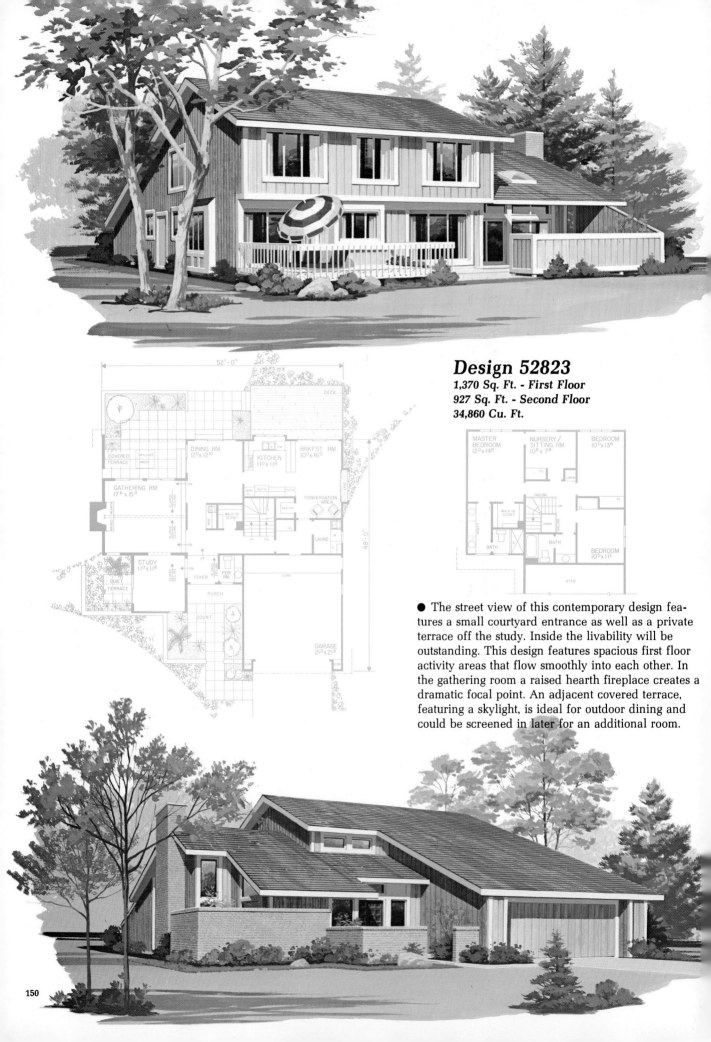

Design 52823
1,370 Sq. Ft. - First Floor
927 Sq. Ft. - Second Floor
34,860 Cu. Ft.

● The street view of this contemporary design features a small courtyard entrance as well as a private terrace off the study. Inside the livability will be outstanding. This design features spacious first floor activity areas that flow smoothly into each other. In the gathering room a raised hearth fireplace creates a dramatic focal point. An adjacent covered terrace, featuring a skylight, is ideal for outdoor dining and could be screened in later for an additional room.

Design 52826
1,112 Sq. Ft. - First Floor
881 Sq. Ft. - Second Floor
32,770 Cu. Ft.

● This is an outstanding example of the type of informal, traditional-style architecture that has captured the modern imagination. The interior plan houses all the features that people want most - a spacious gathering room, formal and informal dining areas, efficient, U-shaped kitchen, master bedroom, two children's bedrooms, second-floor lounge, entrance court and rear terrace and deck. Study all areas of this plan carefully.

ALTERNATE KITCHEN/DINING RM./
BREAKFAST RM. FLOOR PLAN

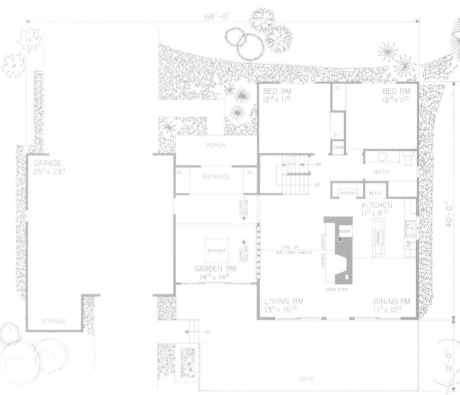

Design 52487 *1,407 Sq. Ft. – First Floor; 833 Sq. Ft. – Second Floor; 35,555 Cu. Ft.*

● This contemporary vacation home will be distinctive at any location. The exterior is highlighted by angled roofs and sweeping expanses of wood and glass. Entrance to the home is through a skylight garden room with sloped ceiling. The living area is adjacent in- cluding a living room, dining room and kitchen. A massive raised hearth fire- place attractively divides the living area from the work center. Access to the large deck will be achieved through sliding glass doors in the gar- den, living and dining rooms. Two bedrooms and a bath are in the rear of the plan. The second floor master bed- room, an additional bedroom and lounge, which overlooks the living areas below, create the final finishing touch to this design. Make this your holiday or everyday home.

MULTI-LEVEL VERSIONS . . . *for flat and hillside*

sites. As with the conventional home, the vacation home can be a split-level, bi-level, or hillside design. It may be called upon to adapt itself to a sloping site. In many cases, merely providing a basement and exposing it can significantly, and economically, increase the livability. Generally, the multi-level nature of these designs lends itself to the development of practical and dramatic outdoor living areas. Decks, balconies and terraces all working together and functioning with the indoor living areas can make the vacation way of life an exciting one, indeed.

Design 52485 1,108 Sq. Ft. - Main Level
983 Sq. Ft. - Lower Level; 21,530 Cu. Ft.

● This hillside vacation home gives the appearance of being a one-story from the road. However, since it is built off the edge of a slope, the rear exterior is a full two-story structure. Notice the projecting deck and how it shelters the terrace. Each of the generous glass areas is protected from the summer sun by the overhangs and the extended walls. The clerestory windows of the front exterior provide natural light to the center of the plan.

Design 52455

864 Sq. Ft. – Upper Level
864 Sq. Ft. – Lower Level; 16,934 Cu. Ft.

Upper Level plan labels:
8'-0" 20'-0" 16'-0" 36'-0"
CARPORT 20⁰ x 12⁰
12'-0"
STORAGE
DECK
4'-0"
BRM. REF'G S. RANGE
ENTRY DN.
KIT. 15⁴ x 9⁰
28'-0"
PANTRY
S. CL. W.R.
SNACK BAR
24'-0"
RAISED HEARTH
WOOD BOX
DINING 13⁰ x 14⁴
LIVING 22⁴ x 15⁸
10'-2"
DECK

Lower Level plan labels:
UNEX.
PDR. RM.
CL. CL.
BATH
S. d. CL.
BATH CL.
UP
AIR COND.
LIN.
CL.
MASTER BED RM. 12⁰ x 15⁴
BED RM. 9⁸ x 11⁶
CL.
BED RM. 10⁰ x 11⁶
COVERED TERRACE

● What delightful vacation living experiences will be in store for the owners and guests of this great second home. Designed for a sloping site, the lakeside elevation has both the upper and lower levels completely exposed for the fullest enjoyment of indoor-outdoor living patterns. The wooden deck, which runs the full length of two sides of the house, is but a step from the upper level living areas. The covered terrace is readily accessible from the lower level bedrooms. The carport with its bulk storage room is located on the same grade as the upper level. The wonderful living-dining area is 35 feet in length. It features sliding glass doors and a strategically placed raised hearth fireplace. Don't miss the snack bar, the wash room, the two full baths and the powder room.

Design 52482
960 Sq. Ft. – Upper Level
622 Sq. Ft. – Lower Level; 17,352 Cu. Ft.

● This home offers its occupants a sunny deck which is accessible from two sets of sliding glass doors in the beamed ceil-inged living room. The dining room plus an informal snack bar are available for eating. Three bedrooms and two full baths to serve the family for sleeping arrangements. The deck acts as a cover for the carport/terrace. A great area when hiding away from the weather is necessary.

Design 52463

624 Sq. Ft. – Main Level; 448 Sq. Ft. – Upper Level
448 Sq. Ft. – Lower Level; 16,232 Cu. Ft.

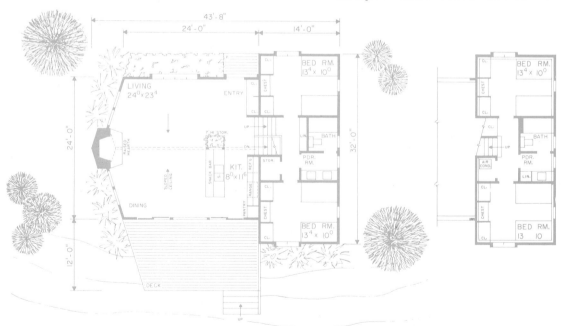

● If you like split-level living there is no reason why your second home can't provide you with those living patterns. If you haven't ever lived in a split-level home, here is your opportunity to do so. The one-story portion of this plan houses the living areas. The two-story section comprises the sleeping zones. Open planning results in a gloriously spacious living, dining and kitchen area. The raised hearth fireplace is strategically located and will be enjoyed from the main living area and even the kitchen. Each of the two sleeping levels features two very good sized bedrooms, a compartmented bath and excellent storage facilities. The use of double bunks will really enable you to entertain a crowd on those glorious holiday weekends. Note built-in chests.

Design 52464
960 Sq. Ft. – First Floor
448 Sq. Ft. – Second Floor; 16,217 Cu. Ft.

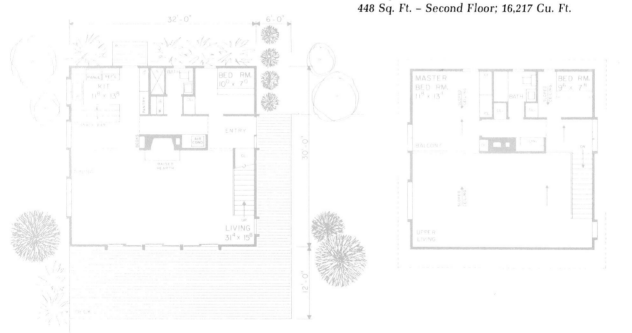

● Almost a perfect square (32 x 30 feet), this economically built leisure home has a wealth of features. The list is a long one and well might begin with that wood deck just outside the sliding glass doors of the 31 foot living area. And what an area it really is – 31 feet in length and with a sloped ceiling! The list of features continues with the U-shaped kitchen, the snack bar, the pantry and closet storage wall, the two full baths (one with stall shower), three bedrooms and raised hearth fireplace. Perhaps the favorite highlight will be the manner in which the second floor overlooks the first floor. The second floor balcony adds even a greater dimension of spaciousness and interior appeal. Don't miss side and rear entries. Observe coat closets placed nearby.

Design 52465
1,144 Sq. Ft. – Upper Level
1,144 Sq. Ft. – Lower Level; 22,651 Cu. Ft.

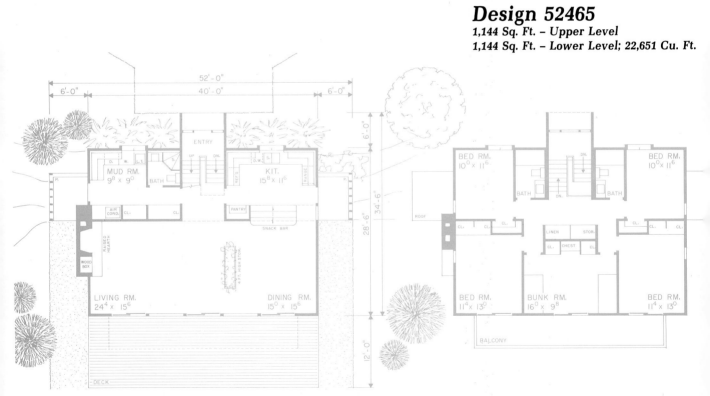

● Here is a ski or hunting lodge which will cater successfully to a crowd. Or, here is a summer home which will be ideal for your own family and an occasional weekend guest. Whatever its purpose, this bi-level design will serve admirably.

And little wonder. There is plenty of space as illustrated by the 29 foot living-dining area, the 15 foot kitchen, the three full baths, the four sizable bedrooms and the large bunk room. In addition, there is the mud room. The features do not end there.

The list continues and includes the raised hearth fireplace, snack bar, planter/storage unit, an abundance of closets, sliding glass doors and a wonderful balcony. Note the two covered side entrances at each end of the house. A great convenience.

Design 52438

977 Sq. Ft. – Upper Level
987 Sq. Ft. – Lower Level; 19,129 Cu. Ft.

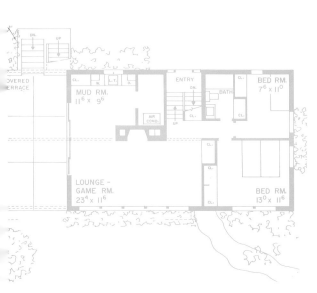

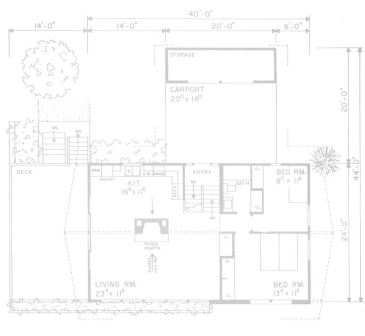

● A great bi-level that could easily be adapted to either a flat or sloping site. As you walk into the main entry beneath the carport, you will either go up a short stairway to the upper main level or down a few stairs to the lower recreation level. In addition to the spa-cious living areas each level features two bedrooms, a full bath, a fireplace, two sets of sliding glass doors and good storage potential. The kitchen of the upper level is efficient and has plenty of space for eating. Directly below is the mud room complete with laundry equipment. The two large outdoor living areas, the deck and terrace, will be favorite spots to soak up the surroundings. Note the sloping ceilings of the living area and kitchen and the bulk storage unit. The lounge-game room will be in constant use.

Design 52403

1,339 Sq. Ft. – Upper Level
1,063 Sq. Ft. – Lower Level; 22,660 Cu. Ft

● If your vacation home site has a view, be sure your choice of design provides you and your family with the opportunity to enjoy it to the fullest extent possible. Projecting from a sloping site this bi-level haven permits a great view from each level. The shed type roof results in sloped ceilings for the living room. Together with all that glass, the fireplace and the outdoor balcony will be everyone's favorite spot. Don't miss the four bedrooms.

Design 52406

1,293 Sq. Ft. – Upper Level
769 Sq. Ft. – Lower Level; 19,918 Cu. Ft.

● For sheer dramatic appeal this two-level, low-pitch roofed contemporary will be difficult to beat. While pictured here oriented on a sloping site, it would adapt well on a flat site. The large living room with its adjacent study enjoys the long wall of glass. With the sloped ceiling, the raised hearth fireplace and such a delightful awareness of the outdoors, this will be a wonderfully cozy area. On the lower level is the family's game room.

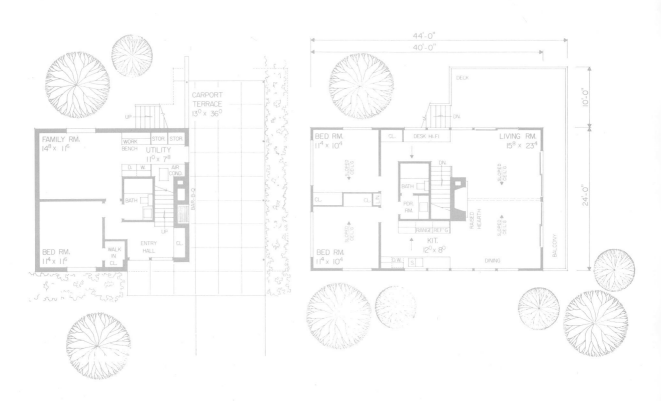

Design 51445
960 Sq. Ft. – Upper Level
628 Sq. Ft. – Lower Level
15,304 Cu. Ft.

● Why not give two-level living a try and make your leisure-time home something delightfully different? If there is plenty of countryside or water around, you'll love viewing it from the upper level. And the best seat in the house will not be inside at all, but one on the balcony or deck. While the upper level is a complete living unit with its two bedrooms, bath, kitchen and spacious living area; the lower level with its one bedroom, bath, utility room (make it a kitchen) and family room could be a complete living unit itself. However called upon to function, this design has plenty of flexible space. Don't miss the fireplace on the upper level.

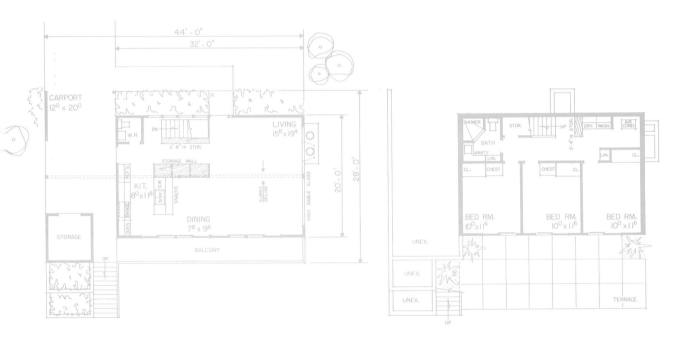

Design 51441
640 Sq. Ft. – Upper Level
640 Sq. Ft. – Lower Level
11,789 Cu. Ft.

● If your vacation home site slopes to the rear you should be looking for a design which will exploit this feature to the fullest. This design will function ideally on such terrain. As a result of the exposed lower level, the resulting extra livable floor area is gained at an amazingly low cost per square foot. One level is the living area. It has a large living/dining area, lots of glass and a balcony which looks down into the lower terrace. An extra wash room, plenty of storage and a snack bar also are present. A fireplace may be incorporated, if desired. The lower level functions as the sleeping area. The laundry equipment and extra storage space is found here.

Design 51465
784 Sq. Ft. – First Floor
434 Sq. Ft. – Second Floor
11,172 Cu. Ft.

● Can you imagine the mounting excitement as your family arrives for the weekend at this distinctive cottage? The joy will be overwhelming as the atmosphere becomes alive with the anticipation of fun. A quick look at this exterior reveals how delightfully different in character it is. A study of the floor plan reveals facilities for joyful living patterns. There are three bedrooms, two full baths, a U-shaped kitchen and a spacious living-dining area. Observe the balcony looking down into the living room. Sliding glass doors permit the living area to function with the deck.

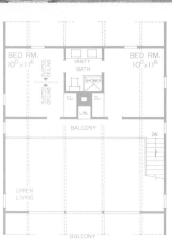

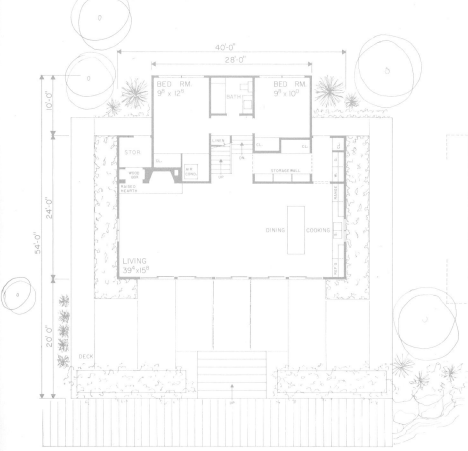

Design 52414
870 Sq. Ft. — Main Level
474 Sq. Ft. — Upper Level
334 Sq. Ft. — Lower Level; 19,902 Cu. Ft.

Design 51437
592 Sq. Ft. – Upper Level
592 Sq. Ft. – Lower Level
10,751 Cu. Ft.

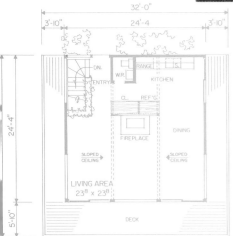

● A compact leisure-time home with plenty of livability and a refreshing exterior. Whether overlooking the lake shore, or perched deep in the woods, the view of the surrounding outdoors will be enjoyed to the fullest. The expanses of glass will permit those inside to be delightfully conscious of nature's beauty. The deck, which envelops the cottage on three sides, will become the favorite spot to enjoy outdoor relaxation.

● Do you think you might like your vacation home to have a light touch of the Oriental flavor? The character of the peaked, wide overhanging roof, to be sure, is refreshing. Completing the setting is the deck and raised planters. The focal point of the interior is the 39 foot living area. The in-line kitchen is at one end with open planning to make available all the dining space the occasion may demand. The wall of windows and the high ceiling further enhances the feeling of spaciousness. From the second floor balcony you can look down into the living area.

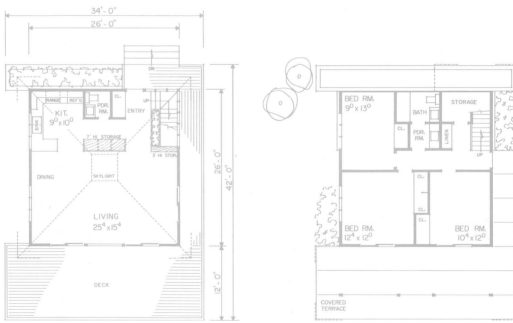

Design 51468 *676 Sq. Ft. – Upper Level; 676 Sq. Ft. – Lower Level; 13,966 Cu. Ft.*

● Vacation living patterns, because of the very nature of things, are different than the everyday living of the city or suburban America. However, they can be made to be even more delightfully so, when called upon to function in harmony with such a distinctive two-level design as this. The upper level is the pleasantly open and spacious living level. The ceilings are sloped and converge at the skylight. Outside the glass sliding doors is the large deck which looks down onto the surrounding countryside. The lower level is the sleeping level with three bedrooms and a full bath. The covered terrace is just outside two of the bedrooms through sliding glass doors.

Design 51466 960 Sq. Ft. – Upper Level; 288 Sq. Ft. – Lower Level; 12,640 Cu. Ft.

● A second home to satisfy your desires for something different both in the way of design and living patterns. This T-shaped home is surely dramatic and unique in its exterior styling and shape. Its pleasing proportion and con-

temporary styling will be a credit to your good taste while satisfying your quest for distinction. Entering the lower level from either the covered terrace or the carport, you go right upstairs to the spacious living area. The

large projecting box bay window provides a dramatic backdrop. Two glass walls, the glass gabled end and the sloped ceilings, help create a most cheerful atmosphere and allow an unrestricted view of the outdoors.

Design 51405

786 Sq. Ft. – First Floor
1,050 Sq. Ft. – Second Floor
15,034 Cu. Ft.

64'-0"

16'-8"

UP
FIREPLACE
RAISED HEARTH
LIVING 31⁰ x 15⁸
DINING
TERRACE
STORAGE
W.R.
W.D.
RANGE
S.
D.W.
KIT. 8⁰ x 15⁸
REF'G.
CL.
ENTRY
UP
CARPORT 12⁰ x 26⁴
TERRACE

DN.
BALCONY
STORAGE
CL.
DRESS. RM.
VANITY
BATH
DRESS. RM.
CL.
BED RM. 15⁸ x 15⁸
BED RM. 10⁴ x 7⁸
CL.
CL.
BED RM. 10⁴ x 7⁸
S.
BATH
DN.
LINEN
BATH
BED 13⁰ x
BALCONY

CL.
DRESS. RM.
BATH
CL.
STORAGE 10⁰ x 7⁴
CL.
UP
ENTRY HALL
CARPORT 32⁰ x 16⁰
COVERED PLAY AREA
DRIVE
TERRACE

32'-0"
8'-0"
24'-0"
8'-0"
BED RM. 7⁸ x 11⁰
BATH
CL.
REF'G.
S.
RANGE
CL.
KIT. 18⁰ x 8⁰
DN.
7 HI STORAGE
CL.
CL.
BED RM. 11⁸ x 10⁴
LIVING 19⁸ x 15⁸
DECK

Design 51401

850 Sq. Ft. – Upper Level
374 Sq. Ft. – Lower Level; 10,137 Cu. Ft.

168

GARAGE
BOAT STOR.
23⁰ x 13⁰

SHOWER

BATH

CL.

AIR COND.

UTILITY RM.

CL.

CL.

CL.

UP

ENTRY HALL

BUNK RM.
6⁸ x 9⁸

BUNK RM.
6⁸ x 9⁸

BUNK RM.
7⁴ x 13⁴

COVERED TERRACE

OPEN TERRACE

34'-4"

34'-0"

44'-0"

BED RM.
11⁴ x 11⁴

BATH

VANITY

MASTER BED RM.
13⁴ x 11⁴

CL.

CL.

LINEN

CL.

CL.

CL.

DN.

SLOPED CEILING

DINING

LIVING
33⁴ x 13⁶

BRM

PANTRY

REF'G

RANGE

KIT.
9⁴ x 12⁰

S.

PASS-THRU

COVERED BALCONY

Design 52433
1,032 Sq. Ft. – Upper Level
636 Sq. Ft. – Lower Level; 17,829 Cu. Ft.

● If yours is a big family, or even a small family which likes to have visitors about, this two level cottage will serve you well. There are two large bedrooms, plus three smaller bunk rooms. There are two full baths, a convenient work center and a 33 foot living area! Certainly the favored spot will be the covered balcony of the upper level. Pass-thru to the kitchen will make the serving of outdoor meals a cinch. Don't miss the utility room and the garage boat storage area.

Design 51498 *768 Sq. Ft. – Main Level; 546 Sq. Ft. – Upper Level; 768 Sq. Ft. – Lower Level; 18,811 Cu. Ft.*

● If it is space you need in your leisure living home, you should give a lot of thought to this multi-level design. It has just about everything to assure a pleasant visit. There are abundant sleeping facilities, fine recreational areas, 2½ baths, an excellent kitchen and good storage potential. The large deck and covered terrace will be popular spots.

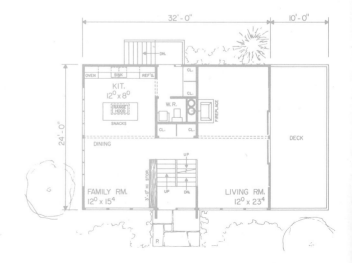

● Finding sleeping space for the weekend gang that often shows up at the cottage, is frequently a major problem. Further, having adequate bath facilities presents an additional problem much of the time. This two-level design does a magnificent job in alleviating these problems to provide trouble-free leisure living. In addition to the four bedrooms, there are two bunk rooms! Two full baths, each with a stall shower and built-in vanity, are convenient to the bedrooms. A third bath is located on the lower level adjacent to the family room. The kitchen area provides plenty of space for eating. Observe the two-way fireplace in the living room plus a fireplace in the family room.

Design 51434

1,376 Sq. Ft. – Upper Level
576 Sq. Ft. – Lower Level
19,902 Cu. Ft.

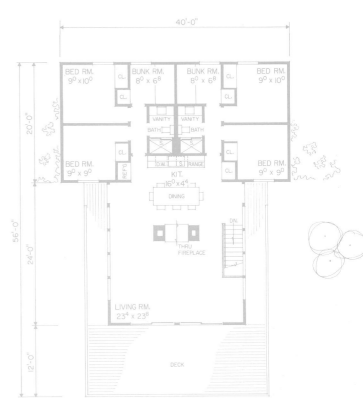

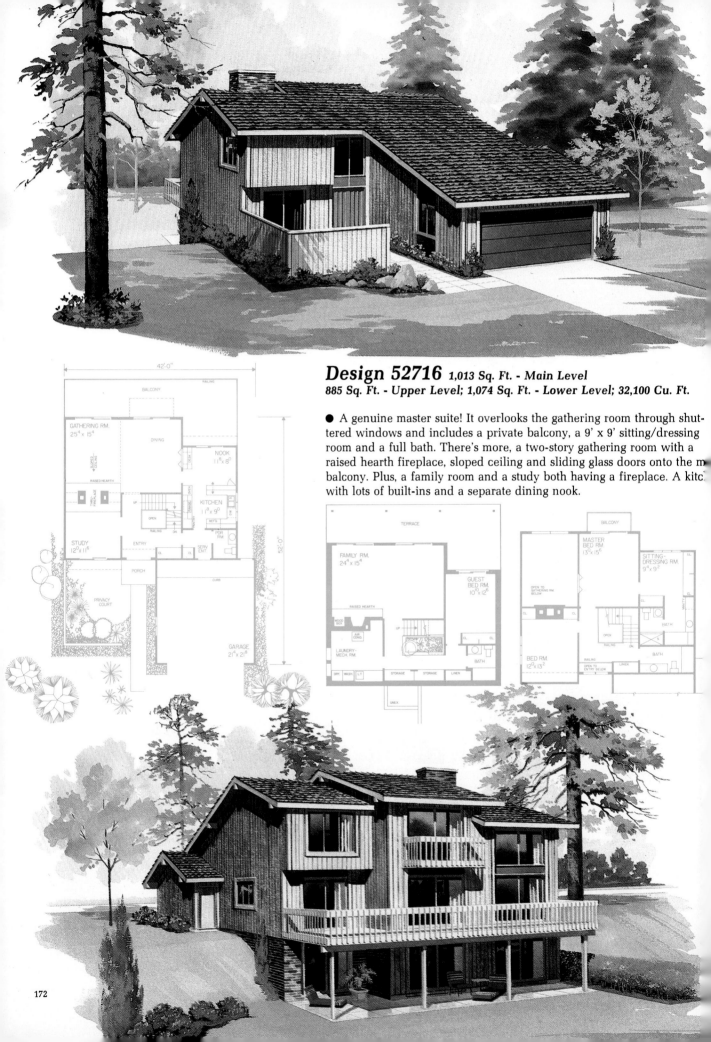

Design 52716 *1,013 Sq. Ft. - Main Level*
885 Sq. Ft. - Upper Level; 1,074 Sq. Ft. - Lower Level; 32,100 Cu. Ft.

● A genuine master suite! It overlooks the gathering room through shuttered windows and includes a private balcony, a 9' x 9' sitting/dressing room and a full bath. There's more, a two-story gathering room with a raised hearth fireplace, sloped ceiling and sliding glass doors onto the m balcony. Plus, a family room and a study both having a fireplace. A kitc with lots of built-ins and a separate dining nook.

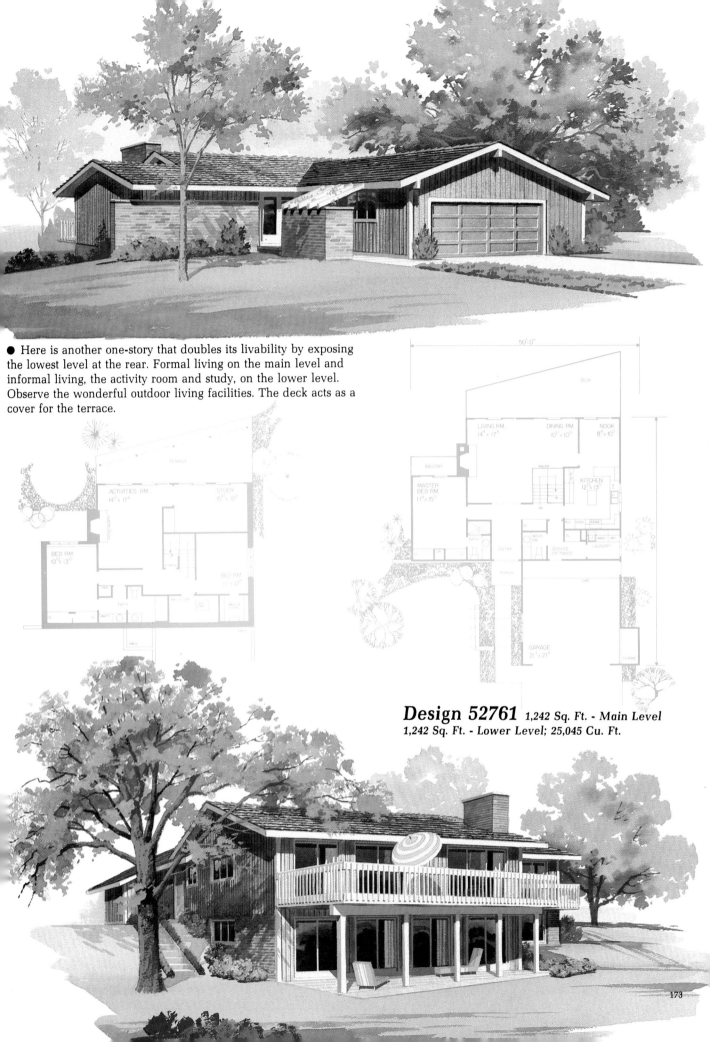

● Here is another one-story that doubles its livability by exposing the lowest level at the rear. Formal living on the main level and informal living, the activity room and study, on the lower level. Observe the wonderful outdoor living facilities. The deck acts as a cover for the terrace.

Design 52761 1,242 Sq. Ft. - Main Level
1,242 Sq. Ft. - Lower Level; 25,045 Cu. Ft.

Design 52842

156 Sq. Ft. - Entrance Level
1,038 Sq. Ft. - Upper Level
1,022 Sq. Ft. - Lower Level
25,630 Cu. Ft.

● This narrow, 42 foot width, house can be built on a narrow lot to cut down overall costs. Yet its dramatic appeal surely is worth a million. The projecting front garage creates a pleasing curved drive. One enters this house through the covered porch to the entrance level foyer. At this point the stairs lead down to the living area consisting of formal living room, family room, kitchen and dining area then up the stairs to the four bedroom-two bath sleeping area. The indoor-outdoor living relationship at the rear is outstanding.

Design 52827 *1,618 Sq. Ft. - Upper Level*
1,458 Sq. Ft. - Lower Level; 41,370 Cu. Ft.

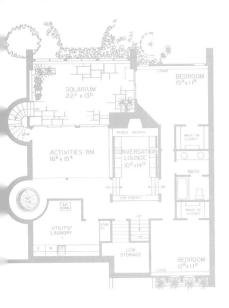

The towering, two-story solarium in this bi-level design
is its key to energy savings. Study the efficiency of this
floor plan. The conversation lounge on the lower level is
a unique focal point.

Design 52435

960 Sq. Ft. – Upper Level
312 Sq. Ft. – Lower Level; 14,026 Cu. Ft.

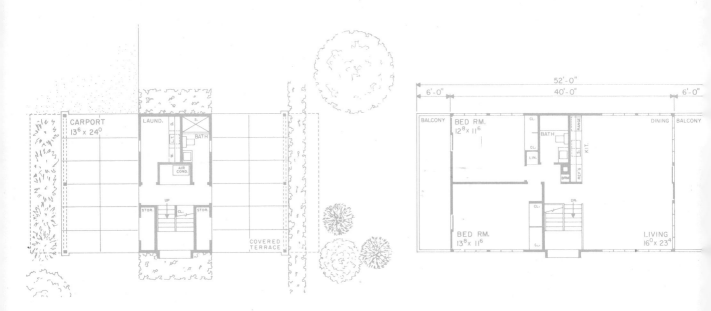

● Make your second home, or retirement home, one that has a distinctive flair. This modified, T-shaped design will be great fun to live in. You'll not have any difficulty enjoying the surrounding countryside from the vantage points as offered here. The projecting bedroom and living wings have their own outdoor balconies. In addition, they cleverly provide the shelter for the carport and the terrace. The lower level features the laundry, the heater room and a full bath with stall shower. The stairway to the upper level features a landing from which a great view of the outdoors can be enjoyed. Upstairs, the byword is spaciousness fostered by the large rooms and all those windows and sliding glass doors. Truly a fine design to be enjoyed by all the family.